# MAN
## OF THE
# HOUSE

# MAN OF THE HOUSE

*Life with the Lady
at the End of My Leash*

MARY & MAC KISER

Published by Mac House Press

Copyright © 2019 by Mary Kiser

First Edition

Mac House Press
P.O. Box 178122
San Diego, CA 92177

www.marykiserwrites.com

Cover & Interior Design: GKS Creative, gkscreative.com

Library of Congress Case Number 1-8117749941

ISBN: 978-1-7331429-0-8 (Ingram Spark paperback)
ISBN: 978-1-7331429-1-5 (KDP paperback)
ISBN: 978-1-7331429-2-2 (ebook)

For media or booking inquiries, please contact:

STRATEGIES Public Relations
P.O. Box 178122
San Diego, CA 92177
858-467-1978
jkuritz@strategiespr.com

First printed in the United State of America.

# Dedication

*In memory of my beloved Mac. You were my sunshine.*

# Table of Contents

# Prologue

My earliest memory is being in a crowded metal pen in a small living room surrounded by four-legged mounds of yellow fur that looked just like me. We didn't have names. We were known by the color of the simple collars buckled around our necks. I was Black and I had to fight Pink, Green, and five other siblings for space at Mama's belly. Mama always looked tired. I felt bad for her but not bad enough to quit eating, a trait I would carry with me throughout my life.

A family named McMillan took care of Mama, and she took care of us. As we started growing more and sleeping less, the McMillans took us out of the house and into their backyard. They'd hold us up in the air and bring our faces down to theirs for a kiss. My short stubby legs moved quickly in an effort to get back on the ground and back to Mama's belly. One day they took her belly away. I cried so much. I'd like to say it was because I missed being close to Mama, but it was because I was hungry. In place of Mama's milk, we were given hard round brown discs called kibbles from a bag. An unsuitable substitute.

One day Mary and Laura came to see us. I'd learned at this early age that people have names instead of colors. They sat on the grass and took turns holding my siblings. I stayed away at first, but curiosity got the best of me. I wandered over to Mary, whose chubby legs were stretched out on the ground cradling Red. I pushed Red out of the way and took her place. Ahh, this was comfortable. I fell asleep until I heard the sound of kibbles in the silver tin bowl.

Mary and Laura watched us eat. Mary wrote something on a piece of paper, gave it to the McMillans and headed straight to me. Then she took me away from the only life I had ever known to a life I would never want to live without.

We got into Mary's car. I didn't know what a car was, and I was scared. The ground moved beneath me. Trees and houses and sky raced past the window. Laura cradled my shaking body in a fluffy fleece pad. I tried to get off her lap but she held me tight. I wanted out.

Little did I know then the impact Mary's car would have on my life. A car ride with Mary meant the possibility of going to the beach or Runyon Canyon or a dog park to play ball or get ice cream! That same car would make me sad at being left behind followed by ecstasy when I heard the garage door open and Mary was back with me where she belonged.

Being scared of something that later made me happy is a recurring theme in life with Mary. For both of us, I think.

The car stopped moving when we pulled into Havenhurst Drive, my new home, where I christened the lawn with runny poop. It didn't feel like home. I missed Mama. I missed my brothers and sisters and the McMillans. It was just me with Mary and Laura.

But it wasn't. My new home was not just a room or a house or a yard. It was a neighborhood. Neighborhoods have sidewalks and bushes and streets and trees and SQUIRRELS. Bushes have wonderful smells and discarded French fries and pizza crust. And there are lots of dogs, not just Labs. There are shepherds and bulldogs and collies and terriers and pit bulls and pugs and dogs that are a mix of all of these.

In addition to my new home, I got a name, a real name, not just a color. Mary named me Mac after the McMillans. I was cool with that. The McMillans were good to me, and when I thought about them, I thought about Mama. Those were good memories.

The only drawback of a neighborhood compared to a back yard is this thing called a leash, a leather strap or rope that "leashers" attach to dogs when we go out of the house. Leashes keep me from catching squirrels and crossing the street when I want to. But without a leash, I couldn't go with Mary to restaurants or church or walk around the city or sit in the park. A leash is not all that bad, as long as Mary is at the end of it.

*I didn't have a dog growing up, nor did I have a strong yearning to get one. When I moved to Los Angeles in my thirties, several friends had dogs. I was enjoying all the fun, sun, and nightlife that the city had to offer and felt sorry for those who had to go home early to feed and walk their dogs. Whenever we planned out-of-town trips, friends with dogs scrambled to find someone to take care of the dogs or just not go. Dogs were expensive. Grooming costs as much as a haircut, and annual vet bills were more than my doctors' visits. Even if I wanted one of my own, I worked late, traveled for my job, and lived in a condo with no yard.*

*I had been living in L.A. almost ten years when my friend Laura moved in with me while she was between jobs. Laura loved dogs and regaled me with stories of Beau Elvis, the Old English Sheepdog she had shared with a past boyfriend. "While I'm living here and not working, it would be a good time to get a dog," Laura coerced. I remained unfazed by her pressure until the week before Mother's Day 2004, when we attended a play at the Ahmanson Theater. I don't remember the name of the play or what it was about. What I do remember is a dog walking out from behind the curtain on the left side of the stage, hopping up on a chaise lounge center stage, and lying there quietly until the scene was over.*

*That was my trigger, and perhaps the reason I later encouraged Mac's acting career. "Ok, let's get a dog," and before I changed my mind, Laura scoured the newspaper (because that's what you did in 2004) and called about a litter of yellow Labrador puppies that would be available the following Sunday, Mother's Day.*

*I wasn't prepared for what I saw when we entered the McMillan's home. It was essentially a big doghouse. The living room furniture was flush against the walls. In the middle of the room was a three-foot-high wire fence. Lady Brittney VI, not looking very ladylike, was lying on her side, exposing her distended belly and raw nipples, the aftermath of recently weaned puppies. She looked exhausted as her eight offspring—in perpetual motion—crawled over her and each other. Mr. McMillan opened a glass sliding door leading to their backyard while his wife opened the gate to the pen and shooed the puppies outside. You could almost see Lady Brittney sigh in relief.*

*A wooden gate in the corner of the yard opened and the McMillan's son and two friends bounded in from baseball practice with grass stains and red dirt on their white pants. They dropped to their soiled knees and played with the puppies until Mrs. McMillan announced there were chicken nuggets in the oven.*

*Laura and I sat down on the ground, grabbing balls of fur as they passed by. The puppies were nameless but each had a different color collar. We took turns cuddling and playing with the precious pups before settling down and observing what they would do on their own. The big boy with the black collar sniffed along the perimeter before coming to rest on my outstretched legs.*

*"I think I've found my dog," I whispered to Laura as not to disturb him. It wasn't love at first sight, but it was an introduction to life-changing love.*

*I named him Mac after the McMillans. Laura said that one-syllable names were good for training, and we both agreed that the name suited him. I liked what it represented. The McMillans put their lives on hold to raise Mac and his litter. Their house wasn't big or fancy, but it was the one that neighborhood kids gravitated to, which is what I envisioned if I would have had children.*

*The first three months were hard on Mac. Everything about his life was different. He slept by himself in a crate. He met dogs that weren't like him. He didn't have a yard, and he had to walk on a leash.*

*The next twelve months were hard on me. I grew closer to Mac than I ever thought possible. I hated leaving him in the morning, and I got home as soon as I could. I dreaded out-of-town business trips. I discovered that a dog makes a home worth going to and makes it harder to leave.*

*I was lucky to have Laura, but I wanted to be the one to care for him. I did what just two years earlier would have been unthinkable, I left my stable career and became an entrepreneur. Laura moved out and Mac took over. He became the Man of the House.*

# Introduction

August of my twelfth year.

"We almost lost him. He's stable now," the boy leasher in the matching blue cotton top and pants tells the female leasher in the white lab coat. That's a *laboratory* coat as opposed to a Labrador's coat. I've received compliments on mine all my life.

I'm in a heated kennel. The sides are metal. The front is clear with a door and two round holes for me to get air. I close my eyes and wiggle my nostrils back and forth. Nothing smells familiar. I detect other dogs in the room but I can't see or hear them. Close by is a glowing box that reminds me of a television, but only numbers and squiggly lines appear on the screen. I'm lying on pillows and I'm covered with blankets. I try to stand but can't. My legs feel like Nerf balls. Big rubber straws are fastened to my chest and my front left paw. I think they are connected to the boring TV. I'm wearing a stretchy white mesh vest. This is odd. Mary has never been one to put clothes on me like we see on Chihuahuas and Yorkies. The material is tight against my chest, like it's holding my heart in.

Oh, I remember now. There is something wrong with my heart. There is a large *two more* on my heart. Mary cried when Dr. Kim told her. The doctor said it wasn't cancer, but that the *two more* would have to come out. I licked Mary's face. She smiled, but she didn't mean it. I tried to hide after that. I don't like to see Mary sad. But there was nowhere to hide in the bare square room with no furniture.

Beep, beep, beep. Make that noise go away. What is it? It sounds like the Thursday trash truck backing up the driveway. Beyond the beeps, leashers are scurrying about and group talking. I can't make out the voices. Is Mary there?

The beeps are changing now, more a buzz than a beep. The numbers on the television screen are falling. The lines stop squiggling. Multiple leashers crowd around my crate. "His blood pressure is 75/45. Paging Dr. Kim. Stat. Paging Dr. Kim."

I see Mary now. She's holding the long green plastic ball launcher. I bring a new yellow tennis ball to her and drop it at her feet. She cradles the ball in the round end of the launcher and heaves it as hard as she can. I'm already in the spot where I knew she would throw it.

I'm waiting for her outside the coffee store. I stare at Mary through the glass door of a place I can't go. Other leashers try to talk to me, but my sights are on Mary. Finally, the door opens, and she hands me the paper cup full of whipped cream that I lick dry.

We're cuddled up on her bed, paw in arm. I'm able to jump on the bed all by myself. I haven't been able to do that in years. She's singing her silly songs. "If you're happy and you know it, wag your tail." My tail swings wildly at the sound of her voice. "You are my sunshine, my only sunshine. You make me happy when skies are gray. You'll never know, Mac, how much I love you…"

I close my eyes. I see darkness. The beeps have stopped.

"…please don't take my sunshine away."

*I make a lot of promises I don't keep. I may not use the word "promise," but the assurance is implied. Most of the broken promises are to myself. "I'll lose thirty pounds before summer. I'll send physical birthday cards again. I'll*

*put my cell phone away at 8:00 p.m. I'll finish writing the book I started."*

*Man of the House: Life with the Lady at the End of My Leash is the fulfillment of this last promise, and it is really hard because my muse is gone.*

*His name was Mac. His species was dog, but he was innately human. He was a child when I needed someone to care for, a partner when being single made me sad, and a loving parent with unspoken wisdom.*

*When he was twelve, Mac survived life-threatening surgery to remove a baseball size tumor on his heart to live another ten months. We were together for thirteen years. I thought we would have a few more.*

*This book is a series of random musings about people and dogs written over a series of years, usually after morning walks or memorable experiences at dog parks. I visualized compiling the stories into a book and driving with Mac cross-country in our white Mazda SUV, going city to city for book signings in pet stores and book stores. We would experience a mix of high-end, dog-friendly hotels and less-fancy motels where the most extravagant amenity was that they left the light on for you. He would be by my side as I read narratives of our life together. His collar would coordinate with my outfit. The audience of like-minded dog lovers would laugh at some and shed a tear at others as the stories resonated with their own canine relationships.*

*I didn't finish the book, and we never took that trip. Laying regret aside, Man of the House is a tribute to Mac, an amazing dog who gave me so much joy, and to the special bond that animal lovers have with their pets.*

# Dog is the
# New Husband

*"He does know he's a dog, doesn't he?"*

— Luann, neighbor without a dog

## Happy Couple

I am the man of the house. I don't earn a living, but I make life worth living. Mary and I aren't married. We don't even have the same number of legs. We just live together and make each other happy. She makes me happy by throwing the tennis ball for an hour. And I make her happy by being happy. I am devoted and loyal.

I am the man of the house. I tell her when it's time to go out and when it's time to eat. I let her know if anyone comes within five feet of the house, and I protect her if they come closer. The things she does for me are not always pleasant, like picking up my poop or washing my leash when I pee on it. I'm also expensive. She spends a lot of money on me at the pet store, even though she doesn't have to.

I'm not like leashers. I don't care if she gains weight, what she wears, or whether she covers the gray in her hair... unless it stops her from taking me for a walk.

I don't ever want to be without Mary. I hope we both live forever.

*Mac, sometimes I look at you and think you are all I need in life to be happy. As we cuddle in bed and I'm tickling you behind the ears, your smile says it all. "Life is simple; this is perfect, you and me." In your eyes, I see unending devotion. You don't speak because you can't, but the unspoken language between us is more descriptive than all the words in Webster's. You plead with me to go outside, and I acquiesce to your request. Still content with our bond, fulfilled with our relationship, we stroll down the street, hand in leash. You tug me in a different direction so you can lick the spot on the lawn where another dog pooped.*

*Reality slaps me in the face like an abusive parent.*

*You are a dog, not a human, not my soul mate, not my lover. You meet many, but not all, of my needs. If only human interaction was as easy as ours, but it isn't.*

*I'm reminded of my needs and desires to meet a man with two legs, preferably one who hasn't been neutered and won't pee on the carpet.*

## Manipulator Extraordinaire

It is so easy to manipulate my leasher, like taking a tennis ball from a terrier. If I want to go outside, I whimper. I start whimpering long before I need to do "doggy business" as she calls it. I whimper because I want to get out of the house and into the street where men with yellow hard hats drop their potato chips. Where the grass has a fresh scent of Caviar (my cute terrier neighbor, not the food). Where we might run into Arrow, a handsome French Bulldog, and his leasher who carries unprotected treats in his pocket. Where life is more interesting than a sofa and a television.

If I want to play ball, I simply pick up a tennis ball and drop it. Sometimes she responds right away but most of the time I have to drop the ball in her lap, which causes her to laugh, squeeze my jowls, and say, "How can I resist that beautiful face?"

I'm pretty damn cute.

I have two methods for getting something to eat. The first is to stand in front of the closet where she keeps my food and stare at the door. If I get no response, I stare into her kind eyes with my pitiful eyes. Then I stare at the door again. I look back and forth between the hard door and soft Mary. That works most every time. The second is to walk out to the kitchen every time I hear the refrigerator door open, which is fairly often. Mary needs to cut back on the kibbles. She rarely eats something without slipping me a treat, too. I don't know if it's because of her manners, compassion, or guilt, and frankly I don't care.

When I want Mary to rub my tummy, I lay on my back on the shag rug in the living room and stretch out my hind legs so that my paws almost touch the wall. I reach my front legs over my head like I'm holding onto an imaginary rope tied to a chair on the opposite side of the room. I wiggle and squirm like I have an itch that needs to be scratched. I look sideways from the corner of my eye to see if she's paying attention. If she's not paying attention, I let out a loud "Ahh" until her red-painted fingernails tickle my belly.

I don't want you to think I'm totally self-absorbed. Sometimes I exploit my puppy dog eyes because of the sorrow I see in hers. That's when I put my chin in her lap and leave it there until she's distracted from whatever is making her sad. I don't pull away when she hugs me tight, even when her tears soak the fur on my neck, because that's when she needs me the most.

## Does He Look Like Me?

*Do people pick dogs that look like them or do people start to look like their dogs after they are together for a while? I can't speak to hairy ears, fading noses, or the desire to lick your feet (and other body parts), but I do recognize a correlation between dog and owner weight and hair color.*

*Nike, a long, lean German shepherd whose rows of ribs poke through her gold, red, and dark-brown coat, is companion to Rose, a tall, lean swimmer. On occasion, when an appointment with her colorist is overdue, Rose, too, has a dark base and strawberry-blonde hair.*

*Viking, the other German shepherd on the street, is fit and solid without an ounce of fat. Different from Nike, his coloring is black, gray, and white. Viking's owner Sandra has the body of an athlete. Sandra's long, dark hair is accentuated with natural gray and intentionally added platinum streaks. I didn't recognize the resemblance until I was talking to a new neighbor about Viking and Sandra, and he asked, "Is that the girl who dyes her hair to match her dog?"*

*Then there's Mac, a natural blonde like me, who would be healthier and more attractive sans the added pounds. I realize it's my fault he's overweight. It's not like he goes to the freezer and opens a new carton of ice cream to find that, moments later, his spoon is scraping the bottom. Nor can he open the cabinet and devour a bag of pretzels without my assistance.*

*I heard an inspirational speaker scream, as they often do, about the ludicrous manufacturing of diet food for dogs. "People, don't feed the dog more food than he needs. How simple is that?" he shouted.*

*I suppose it should be simple, for both of us, actually. But it isn't. Hunger is rarely the reason I eat.*

*I eat when I'm sad, when I'm lonely, and to delay doing something I don't want to do. I even eat to avoid things I actually like to do, like exercising or writing. The fear of failure or imperfection paralyzes me, and*

*I eat instead of tasting life.*

*My emotional eating is contagious, and Mac suffers. I feel guilty eating in front of him and I feel sorry that he can't get food anytime he wants. So, when I eat, he gets a little treat, too.*

*His keen senses don't help the situation. Mac has supersonic hearing when it comes to the refrigerator door. He can be in an upstairs bedroom asleep with the door closed, but when I access the appliance, he magically appears by my side with eyes sad enough to make a villain cry. It's impossible to resist the hungry expression on his lovable face. Impossible for me, that is.*

*My friend Sandra tells a story about a night Mac stayed with Viking and her. "Mac would stand in front of my refrigerator and look longingly from the refrigerator to me with the most pitiful look on his face. Mac, give it up. That routine doesn't work on me."*

*In the argument of nature versus nurture, it appears nurture is the dominating factor in human and canine couples. The onus is on me to make sure Mac and I are lean and have great hair.*

## Mac as Judge?

*I read in the Los Angeles Times that Candy Spelling, widow of the late Hollywood producer Aaron Spelling, sold her 100-room Los Angeles mansion for $150 million. As Mac would say, "That's a lot of tennis balls." The article gave an interesting account of her selection process for hiring a Realtor to manage the listing. Candy instructed her security staff to escort a prospective Realtor into the house while she observed the way her dog reacted to the guest.*

*Now come on. I love my dog, and Mac is smart. I rely on him for many things, but I don't believe he has the wherewithal to negotiate a $150 million transaction. The Realtor could be ignorant, inexperienced, and unethical, but would be Mac's first choice if he had the lingering aroma of the morning's breakfast bacon on his pants.*

*However, like Mrs. Spelling, I am intrigued by the way Mac responds to people. On this morning's walk, an unshaven man in dirty khakis with a filthy plaid blanket wrapped around his torso struck up a conversation with us. He showered attention on Mac, scratched under his chin, and said, "Good boy Old Yeller" in a gruff voice ravaged by years of cigarette smoke. Mac lifted his chin, closed his eyes, and wagged his tail in sweet response.*

*Paradoxically, Mac growls at Lada, our Russian neighbor who is lovely and sweet and a talented violinist. Lada's generally not afraid of dogs, but she is afraid of Mac, which breaks my heart because I want him to be kind to kind people.*

*They say dogs are a good judge of character, but Mac has been crazy about men in my life who later turned out to be real scumbags. Mac loved Christian, whom I trusted not only with my love and friendship, but with my money. Christian was deserving of none of these and disappeared with all of them.*

*I suppose a dog's heart can be fooled, too.*

*Anyway, Candy got $150 million for her house in the worst financial* *market since the Great Depression, so I guess her dog did a good job. What next? Should Mac select my dry cleaners, dentist, gynecologist?*

## Working Dogs

Woody is a black Lab puppy who lives on my street. But he's only going to live here for a year. Then he goes to live with a leasher who doesn't know how to see.

Woody has a blue vest with lots of patches. When he wears it, he doesn't get to play with me. He has to sit while our leashers talk. Even if I drop my tennis ball beside him, he's not allowed to pick it up. If a squirrel runs up a tree where we're standing, he doesn't get to chase it.

As if giving up playtime isn't bad enough, he has to give up his leasher when the year is over. It makes my heart sad to think I would only get to live with Mary for a year.

I don't want a blue vest.

*I don't know why I can't accept Mac for the lovable dog that he is. I'm always trying to make him something more.*

*I thought about making Mac a therapy dog and taking him to nursing homes to bring joy and comfort to the residents. Since Mac tends to growl at people with gray hair who walk slowly, I had to rethink that. He would have looked so cute in a baby-blue service vest.*

*My neighbor Bob got an adorable black Lab puppy named Woody. Woody will live with Bob for a year. After that, he will go through an intense training program before being paired with a blind owner. I give Bob lots of credit for doing this, but I would not have been able to give Mac away after having him for a year. I consider myself a fairly unselfish person, but not when it comes to Mac.*

*Since I seem insistent on giving Mac a career, a therapist seems appropriate.*

*When I talk to him about a problem, he looks intensely interested, allowing me to continue talking while I work it out myself. I ask him questions about the direction our lives are taking, and he tilts his head as if to say, "Why do you worry so much?"*

*When I'm sad, Mac lays his chin on my knee. We stare at each other in silence, and my depression dissipates.*

*Mac is my Prozac.*

## The Black Box

I saw Mary take the black box out of the office closet. I hate the black box. She's taking clothes out of her drawers and closet and putting them in the black box. She's going to leave soon. She always does when the box comes out.

Sometimes when the box comes out, Mary sends me to Sadie's house. Sadie, a Golden Retriever, was my first girlfriend. I fell in love with her when she taught me to swim. I like going to Sadie's house because she has a pool. I don't like going there without Mary.

Sometimes Laura will come to our house when Mary and the black box leave. Laura is a special leasher who I've known since I was a puppy. I love Laura a lot, but she's not Mary. She keeps me awake at night and doesn't take me on long walks in the morning.

I'm sad. I don't like the black box. It means Mary doesn't love me. I don't want to live without her. Why go on? I drop to the floor with my head on my paws. My eyes bore into the floor. Will I ever see her again? Or will the black box take her away from me forever?

*I try to hide my suitcase from Mac. I can't stand the look in his eyes when he sees me pull it out of the closet. Usually I try to pack when he's already where he's going to stay while I'm away or when he's asleep in the corner of the sofa, where he knows he's not supposed to be. But this time there's no hiding it.*

*I didn't know I'd be pulling out the suitcase again so soon. I didn't know my brother-in-law Jerry was going to die from a heart attack yesterday and I would have to pack dresses, stockings, and heels and go back to Virginia just two weeks after I was there.*

*I don't like pulling out the suitcase because it makes Mac sad, but it's not the issue this time. He's been sad all day. He's seen me cry and wipe the reapplied black mascara that smears my face each time I tell someone about Jerry.*

*Mac's ignoring me now, and I know he's hurting. Why do we turn away from those we love when we need them most? Typically, happiness and strength are considered "good" while sadness and weakness are "bad." We don't want others to see us being weak or sad, but what we don't realize is that comforting us with their strength gives them a chance to be good.*

*When someone dies, people not only feel sad, they feel helpless since nothing they do or say changes the permanency of death. What Mac can't understand is that this trip is not like others where I've traveled for business or vacation. I need his comfort. Or maybe he understands more than I think, and he feels helpless too.*

## Labels

Everyone calls me a Momma's Boy. The way they say it doesn't sound like a compliment. People don't understand how much I love Mary. She feeds me, takes me on long walks, buys me toys, plays ball with me, gives me treats, rubs my tummy, and sleeps with me. It's only the two of us, and that's the way I want it. Don't get me wrong. I like meeting other leashers and their dogs, but I get tired of them easily. After a scratch from a random leasher and a few sniffs of their dog, I'm ready to have Mary to myself. I like it when other people come to our house, especially when they come to watch a movie and eat dinner. The more people come, the more dried pizza left in the box on the kitchen counter.

People tell Mary that I have "separation anxiety." They started saying this when I tore up the pillows on the sofa while Mary was gone. I didn't do this because I was anxious. I did it because it was fun. There were too many pillows on the sofa anyway. As I got older, this game wasn't as fun anymore, so I stopped. Because I speak loudly to Mary when she gets home, leashers think I'm anxious. I'm not. I'm trying to tell her the mailman rang the buzzer and left a package, that the gardeners watered the grass, and that I'm so hungry I'm sure malnutrition has set in.

Why do we have labels? They're good for knowing Alpo from Fancy Feast, but "Momma's Boy" and "Separation Anxiety"? Why can't they call it what it is? Love.

*According to DogPsychologyHelp.com, up to 35 percent of dogs suffer from separation anxiety. Yes, such a site does exist. What it doesn't provide are statistics showing how many people suffer from separation anxiety from dogs. I call this SAD for short.*

1.  *If you've ever turned down a dinner invitation at a five-star restaurant, you may be SAD.*

2.  *If you've ever left at the end of the first overtime at a Lakers game, you may be SAD.*

3.  *If you've ever declined an invitation to your grandmother's 100th birthday celebration in another state, you may be SAD.*

4.  *If you've ever let a coupon for an all-expense-paid trip to Hawaii expire, you may be SAD.*

5.  *If you've ever gotten to a New Year's Eve party after 11 and left before midnight, you may be SAD.*

6.  *If you've ever given away your front-row ticket to a sold-out U2 concert, you may be SAD.*

7.  *If you've ever told someone you had to pick up your baby at daycare and you have no children, you may be SAD.*

*Jeff Foxworthy, if you're reading this, and I hope you are, my apologies.*

## And the Winner is...

*A few years ago, when Mickey Rourke accepted a Golden Globe for Best Actor in a Motion Picture Drama, he thanked the customary friends, colleagues, and agents. Then he said something I've not heard in an acceptance speech. He thanked his dogs for being there for him when no one on two legs was.*

*I get that. Although I have friends who are there for me when I need them, something, or rather someone, is missing. Having great friends and a loving family are not enough anymore. I want a partner. I want someone to sit across the dinner table from. I want someone with whom I can explore the grocery store, the city, the world. I want someone's hand to hold in church. I want his body next to mine when I go to bed and when I wake up. I want someone who is equally comfortable in a tux at a black-tie event as he is in sweats walking on the beach at sunset. I want someone who I can talk to for hours or sit comfortably with in silence. I want someone who enjoys my friends but looks forward to time alone with me.*

*Poor Mac. Because there is no man in my life, he is forced to be that partner. For someone who doesn't talk, drive, cook, or earn an income, he does a damn good job. Just like friends and family can't fulfill the need a partner can, neither can Mac. But for all his efforts, the Golden Globe for Best Canine in a Human Role goes to my very own Golden Labrador.*

# Friends in Low-To-The-Ground Places

*"The beautiful thing about the animal community is, it breeds good people. Pets break down the barriers that keep people apart."*

—Hank L.'s Leasher

## Dog Houses

My street has two sidewalks, three fire hydrants and 54 trees. There are six pools on the street, but I can't get to them because they're behind locked gates. If only I could climb fences like those stupid cats, I could go swimming.

There is a tall white building on the street named The Colonial House. My friends Caviar, Nike, Talula, Buster, and Charlie live there with their leashers.

Caviar is a Cairn terrier who barks at most other dogs. He doesn't bark at me, so I feel special.

Nike is an elderly German shepherd who teaches us younger dogs how to slow down and enjoy the grass.

Talula is a small black-and-white Maltese. Her fur falls into her eyes unless her leasher puts a barrette in her hair.

Buster and Charlie are Jack Russell Terriers from the same mother at different times. They have more energy than Caviar, Nike, Talula, and me put together.

The Colonial House is a famous place. Twice a day vans of people I've never seen before with funny shirts and cameras around their necks take pictures of it. The man driving the van talks loudly and tells everyone about the *"Betty Davis unit."* I don't know who she is, so she must not have a dog.

Next to The Colonial House is Mi Casa. Leashers like to name their houses. A sign out front says it's on the historical register, which means it's old and cool and can't be torn down. It can't be all that cool because dogs can't live there.

The building next to Mary and me is called The Jefferson. No one lived there for a while, but two nice ladies bought it and fixed it up for dogs and their leashers. Sammy, Sullivan, Lola, and Gracie live there.

Sammy is a tan pug with a black face and black ears. I think pugs are Labs in short bodies with big eyes. We like the same things and don't bark at too much in life.

Mary calls Sullivan my long-lost cousin because we're both yellow Labs. I see the resemblance.

Lola is a sweet light-eyed Lhasa Apso mix. Both Lola and Sullivan live with teeny tiny baby leashers. Lola and Sullivan said the babies keep them awake at night, but on the positive side, the babies drop a lot of Cheerios and have some fine-smelling poop.

Gracie is a beautiful but timid brown-and-white pit bull. It took a long time for her to look at me. Whenever I tried to smell her butt, she crawled between her leasher's legs. Now we are good friends, but Gracie still doesn't let Mary pet her. Leashers say pit bulls are mean, but I think they're sweet. I make a special effort to say hello to them on the street to make up for leashers who don't.

On the other side of my building is Palmdale House where Dillon, a Lassie impersonator, lives. It's painted green and looks like a ship. The nice man who always called me "Max" lived there before he died. Mary never corrected him when he called me Max.

Across from Dillon's house is Sunset Tropical, a square gray building where Boots lives. Boots is a Yorkie terrier who likes me but growls at Mary. Boots divides his time between two leashers. He's so high maintenance that it takes two leashers to care for him.

Haven Villa is at the end of the street where Pepper lives. Pepper is a black Pug with a pretty leasher named Patty. Mary likes Pepper and Patty a lot because they remind her of her favorite candy.

My house is called LaPrada. That's where Homer and I live. Homer is a gray-and-brown Lhasa Apso /Shih Tzu mix who lives with his leasher, Mark. He doesn't say much because he's old. His number one priority is finding food that I and the other dogs miss.

Two cats also live in LaPrada. If I ever get my paws on them, I'm going to… you know, I really don't know what I'm going to do because I've never been able to see one up close.

I could go on and on because the houses and the dogs do. But I'll stop for now because I need to pee and it takes a while to decide which of the 54 trees I want to tap.

🐾 🐾 🐾 🐾

*Because I grew up in the country where the closest neighbor was three to four cornfields away, living in a close-knit community is all the more special. When I describe the friendships and interactions of my neighbors, other Angelenos find our camaraderie unique and fortuitous.*

*I've said it before but it bears repeating, dogs bring people together. Our block is lined with multi-family units, some apartments, some condos. Most don't have yards, so walking is required to exercise our dogs and accommodate their potty practices. Dogs being dogs, owners are obliged to wait while dogs do what they do, so why not strike up conversation?*

*One thing that makes our neighborhood thrive is what I refer to as "Millionaires and Rent Control." The street is a mixture of old historic properties, new architectural buildings, and older (some quaint, some not so much) rent-controlled apartments. I love the diversity this creates, giving me the opportunity to discuss opera with Dillon's Dad, horse racing with Caviar's Mom, and what's on sale at Target with Homer's Dad.*

*I have deep relationships with some neighbors and some I know through more basic conversations. Little Bill, the short man with no car who walked everywhere called Mac "Max." I didn't see the need to correct him and never did. Bill loved movies, particularly the early age of Hollywood, and could talk for hours if you gave him the time.*

*"Have you seen One Night of Love?" he would ask.*

*"No."*

*"Oh Mary, it's a beautiful romantic musical film set in the opera world, starring Grace Moore and Tullio Carminati. Grace Moore was the original Mimi in La Bohème. It was nominated for Best Picture in 1934 but it got beat by It Happened One Night with Clark Gable and Claudette Colbert. Did you ever see Claudette in Cecil B. Demille's Cleopatra?"*

*And on he would go.*

*I enjoyed the stories and felt guilty when I didn't have time to listen and crossed to the other side of the street to avoid him. I didn't see Little Bill for a few days and neither did anyone else. When his rent was past due, something that had never happened in the 24 years he lived in the rent-controlled building, his landlord checked in on him and found him dead in his bed. I hope he died watching an appropriate Academy award-winning movie like 7th Heaven, Heavenly Music, or Death Becomes Her.*

## Cardiff

My friend Cardiff lives down the street in a building with no name. Cardiff is a small Welsh terrier with curly black-and-brown hair. He looks like a stuffed animal I had as a puppy. But don't let his cuteness fool you. For a dog with short legs, he's quite the jumper and has been known to out-jump me for a dried chicken breast. But the coolest thing about my friend is that he has his own line of dog food called *Cardiff's Crunchies*. They taste yummy, and Cardiff's picture is on the package.

Cardiff has two leashers. Peter is a vet. But he's not like other vets. I don't go to a building with cold floors and sick dogs to see him. Peter comes to my house. He sits down on the carpet and we play. He rubs my body and makes me feel good. His hands are soft and feel like love. I like Peter a lot until he tells Mary not to let me have pigs' ears, bully sticks, or my favorite food from a can. No wonder Cardiff had to create his own dog food.

Paul is Cardiff's second leasher. Paul likes to pick things up. He picks up newspapers that boys on bikes throw in our yards. He also picks up poop other leashers don't. I guess Paul got tired of picking up other dogs' crap. He put a camera in his window. Now when leashers leave poop in their yard, Paul prints a picture of the bad leasher and tapes it to the trees on our street. I guess leashers don't like having their pictures on trees because they don't leave poop on the lawn anymore.

*One of the greatest joys of having a dog is getting to know your neighbors. I met Peter and Paul through their dog, Cardiff. Peter, an integrative veterinarian, combines Eastern and Western medicine to treat*

*his four-legged clients. He makes house calls and, in a town where celebrities value their dogs and their privacy, he maintains a patient list of exclusive clientele.*

*Peter has a gentle bedside manner that is loved by both his patients and their owners.*

*On the other side of the sensitivity scale is Paul. Paul installed a "Poop Cam" in his window facing the street to catch people who neglect to pick up their dogs' excrement. I don't blame him since his grassy front yard is the envy of dogs and owners on Havenhurst.*

*When poop is left on the lawn, he reviews the tapes and prints a still of the irresponsible owner. If he knows where they live, he knocks on their door, hands them the pictures, and says matter-of-factly, "Please pick up your dog's poop or I'll call the police." If he doesn't know them, he tapes a picture of the "poopatrator" on trees lining each side of the street with the caption, "If you know this person, tell them to pick up their poop."*

*Peter and Paul are the Batman and Robin of Havenhurst, keeping our pets healthy and our streets clean.*

## Romancing Ella

I am lucky in love. Mary is my leasher love and Ella is my dog love. Ella is a fluffy gray-and-white husky mix with piercing blue eyes. I loved her the first day I saw her, smelled her, touched her, tasted her, and heard her whimper. I wanted to cry when her leasher told us she almost got hit by a car on a big road.

I love Ella with all my senses.

Each strand of her long fur has a different, yet delicious smell. I feel her presence before I see her. I run in a direction for no reason at all, and there she is.

I think I scare her with my intensity. I run up to Ella, stretch out and spread my two front legs in front of me, put my head on the ground, and stick my butt in the air. My sexy pose and teasing bark challenges her to come and get me. She lies still in the grass. I whine for a response. Her eyes look over me, but she doesn't turn away. I lean down and lick her sweet lips.

My heart beats faster than a new tennis ball bouncing on a wooden floor.

Mary and Jeff, Ella's leasher, laugh at my antics. Mary pulls me away. I don't want to go. But it's good that I do. I don't want Ella to see my heart beat out of my chest.

*I've never seen anything like it. Mac likes other dogs, but he loves Ella. Whenever he sees her, if I let go of the leash, he sprints toward her with lightning speed uncharacteristic of his usual slow morning stride.*

*Once he comes to a screeching halt before his love, he bows down, front legs spread eagle and his rear in the air. She feigns disinterest. He barks to get her attention. It's a bark he only uses for Ella. It's a combination*

27

*between a bark, a cry, and a whimper. He kisses her, runs in circles, and kisses her again. It's like he's possessed.*

*I am truly baffled by Mac's behavior. He only does it around Ella, and he does it every time he sees her.*

*I'm jealous, not of Ella, but of the intensity of Mac's desire for her. I want to find someone who stirs inside me what Mac feels every time he sees Ella.*

## Max and the Anti-Max

*"Can you do me a big favor?" Trent asked. "I'm on my way to L.A. for a couple meetings. Can you keep Max and Cane for the day?" My day was flexible and I hadn't met Max's adopted brother Cane, so I agreed.*

*"Great, I'll be there in 15 minutes."*

*Trent is from Santa Barbara, less than two hours away if there's no traffic and more than four hours away if there is. Max, a chocolate Lab, is a few years older than Mac. He is easy going and acquiesces to whatever Mac wants, whether it's a toy or my affection. I wondered if Cane would change this dynamic.*

*Trent recently adopted Cane from an organization that trains seeing-eye dogs. Trent didn't like his given name and changed it to Cane after ample debate regarding its spelling. Trent considered the biblical "Cain" but upon further research, found that Cain murdered his brother Abel and didn't think this boded well as a sibling for Max. Besides, in naming a dog intended for a blind person, Cane seemed comically appropriate.*

*After 30 seconds with Cane, I understood why he didn't make it as a seeing-eye dog. Cane entered the house like a storm, leaving the room with remnants of toys and splashes from an emptied water bowl. He circled the living room twice before bounding up the stairs, sounding like thunder as his strong athletic legs took the steps two at a time. He made a U-turn at the top of the stairs and returned in a flash.*

*Forget any biblical or blind-man reference; Cane was short for "Hurricane."*

*"Cane," I called. Upon hearing my voice (seemingly for the first time), he stopped and walked slowly to the sofa where I was sitting and placed his sturdy head in my lap. I petted the bridge of his nose and gave him a kiss. He melted at my feet.*

*The eyes of the "Hurricane" closed, and he slept like a baby, gathering energy to unleash the next storm.*

❋ ❋ ❋ ❋

It started out like any other day. Mary reading, me stretching, breakfast, long walk, her at her desk, and then the doorbell rang. I thought it might be the man in the brown pants and shirt Mary likes, but far from it. They were brown alright, but they weren't delivering anything but trouble.

Mary opened the door and in ran Max, a sweet older chocolate version of me. Max doesn't live in my city. Mary and I spent the night with Max and his leasher Trent one time at their house with a big hole in the yard. Trent said they were putting in a pool. I wonder if the hole is a pool yet. Max and I play well together because he is slower than me and I get to the balls first.

Today, there was another dog with Trent and Max named Cane. Cane came in the house first, dragging his leasher behind him. Cane, is also a chocolate Lab. He probably weighs as much as me but is taller and firmer. I know for one thing that he is stronger and wilder. Within seconds, he took all my toys out of the toy basket, drank all my water, and got Mary's attention. That's usually reserved for me.

Trent handed Max and Cane's leashes to Mary and left almost as quickly as he was dragged into the house. I looked at Max with panic in my eyes. The look in his eyes said, "Now you see what I have to live with every day. I'm glad I have someone to help me absorb his energy. But don't worry, it gets easier. He's a sweet dog. Kinda dumb. But sweet."

I have no choice but to trust Max… and hope Trent comes back soon.

## Danes and Confused

*I thought I was back in Virginia fields tending to cattle, but I'm in the middle of West Hollywood at Zach and Bart's house lovingly named "The Fur Patch." Galloping around the yard are five Harlequin Great Danes. White with large black spots, they look like overgrown Dalmatians or undergrown Holstein cows. Joining the Harlequins are four black Great Danes and a lone, lovely, brown lady Dane named Stella.*

*Zach used to live on my street, and I always thought he was a cat person. Depending on whether one had died or how many strays he'd taken in, there were typically two to five cats in his apartment. Zach's standing as a cat person changed the day Storm rolled in.*

*Officially a Blue Dane, Storm has a dark shiny gray coat and light blue eyes. At twenty months old, she is over her awkward stage and is regal and stately in her lean eighty-pound frame. Zach drove eighteen hours to Colorado to pick up Storm when she was eight weeks old. A year later, he made the trek again with his roommate, Bart, to pick up Storm's half-brother, Quake, a Harlequin Dane. Apparently two Danes were not Great enough, so they bought Quake's brother as a gift for their friend Danny. This unexpected gift would become Trooper, the love of Danny's life.*

*The Danes soon outgrew the apartment on Havenhurst, so Zach and Bart bought a house and moved Storm, Quake, four cats, and themselves into a charming home with an even more charming backyard.*

*Zach's move was bittersweet. He had been my neighbor the entire time I lived in West Hollywood, and I was going to miss him and his menagerie. On the bright side, they weren't moving far and offered Mac and me a standing invitation to play in their yard. I'd always wanted a backyard for Mac, where I could sit in a lawn chair and not worry where he was, where we could play ball without competition from fifty other dogs like at the dog park.*

*After moving to The Fur Patch, Zach started a Facebook group called "Danes and Confused," opening up his yard on Sunday evenings for owners to bring their Great Danes for play dates. It's Tinder for big dogs. Mac and a few other non-Great Danes are grandfathered into the club.*

*So today we arrive, bottle of wine in hand, to enjoy a relaxing afternoon in the backyard with the dogs.*

*Wrong!*

*We open the gate of the white picket fence and take five steps up to the front door where a sign reads, "Door is open. Come on in." Mac and I pass a cat spread out on the living room sofa. Surprisingly Mac walks on by. I put the bottle of Chardonnay in the refrigerator, and we make our way through the house to the sliding glass door leading into the backyard. As I slide open the door, ten Great Danes charge us. I fall over as Mac escapes through the table-sized legs of a 180-pound black Great Dane show dog named Navar.*

*A relaxing afternoon gives way to rousing entertainment as owners of un-neutered Danes struggle to keep their children apart. Poor Mac decides against the adage "If you can't beat them, join them," and spends his time sniffing the outer edge of the enclosed yard trying to be invisible.*

*After being knocked to the ground again by a herd of Danes, I say my goodbyes, pry Mac away from the fence, and leave the party before this "Dame" gets a concussion.*

I have a newfound compassion for Yorkies and Chihuahuas. I'm bigger than most of the dogs on my street. I can usually tell when a small dog is scared of me, so I approach calmly. Sometimes I lie on the ground and let them approach me.

Someone needs to teach Storm and Quake's friends this technique. I was so excited to see my Dane friends who moved from our street to a house with a yard. I've known Storm and Quake and their brother Trooper since they were smaller than me. Even when they outgrew me, they were lovable and calm, like gentle giants.

This afternoon at The Fur Patch was strange. I should have known something was different about the day when I saw a cat that didn't want to be chased. In hindsight, the kitty was probably exhausted.

When I tried to enter the backyard, ten monsters charged me. I wanted to smell Quake, Trooper, and Storm, but all I could see was forty legs surrounding me like a forest full of moving tree trunks. Trooper, with his one blue eye and one brown eye, saw the fear in my two brown eyes. He blocked and tackled the others until I could make it to the sidelines of the yard.

Luckily, another Great Dane came to the door. Their simple minds got distracted and I was no longer their target.

I spent the rest of the time trying to be invisible, which wasn't hard amongst a thousand pounds of dogs. Mary either got my drift or got tired of playing dodge Dane and retrieved my leash, motioning to go.

When we got home, Boots was in our driveway. I jumped from the car and ran to say hello.

It sure is good to be the big dog again.

## Courage

*Mac, I hope you are having fun at the ranch. I am with Laura at her brother's house in Louisiana. You would love it here. With a pool in the backyard and a river running along the property, you would never be dry.*

*Laura's family has two dogs. They are not like you, though few (if any) dogs are. The dogs live in an enclosed yard and probably have never been on a sofa, bed, ottoman, or chaise lounge like the ones you assume I purchased for your comfort.*

*Napoleon is a ten-year-old golden retriever with matted fur and a limp. Courage is a muscular black Lab about your age.*

*Courage has a strange trait. Instead of chasing a ball and returning it to me, he fetches his food bowl. When I arrived last night, I went out to see the dogs. As soon as I walked into the yard, Courage brought me his bowl.*

*"I guess it's time to feed the dogs."*

*"He wants you to throw it," replied Laura's nephew, Lance.*

*"Throw what?"*

*"The bowl."*

*Hesitantly, I tossed the dirty metal dish, but it was so heavy that it landed only a few feet from where I was standing. Courage ran to the bowl, which had settled upside down on the grass. With his right front paw, he dug into the ground under one side of the bowl to force it onto its side, grabbed the rim in his mouth, trotted the short distance back to me, and dropped it at my feet. He sat down and looked at me with begging eyes to do it again.*

*This time I drew my arm behind my body and tossed it like an Olympic discus thrower. The bowl soared through the air and bounced once before Courage caught it in waiting jaws. Courage was so fast I almost hit him! As heavy as the bowl was, I think it would have knocked him out. This game continued until my arm ached from the weight of the dish and the repetitive movement.*

*"What made him start chasing his bowl?" I asked Lance.*

*"It all started when he lost the tennis ball we gave him."*

*Thinking about the basket full of tennis balls I keep for you in the hallway closet, I thought to myself, "Why didn't you get him another tennis ball?"*

*The life of a city dog is radically different than the life of a country dog. As I watch Courage roll around in the mud beside his four-by-four-foot dog house, I wonder which of you would have the most fun if the roles were reversed.*

*In my heart, I want to think you have the best life. But in my head, I fear that it's Courage.*

## The Name Behind the Dog

*There are lots of books on what to name a child, and I thought a clever idea for my second book would be to write a book on what to name your dog. That plan ended quickly once a Google search found at least two books already published, one with 5,000 names and one with 1,000 names. I figure 6,000 are enough to choose from, so why compete?*

*I find it interesting how dogs get their names. Some are obvious, like "Oreo," the white Jack Russell with large black spots we met at the park. And like "UB," a Shih Tzu mix with an obvious underbite.*

*Caviar was named as such because he cost so much. Nike was named after the Greek Goddess of Victory, which proved to be true as she fought and won so many battles over death.*

*My friend Ron named his chocolate Lab Sammy Jo after Heather Locklear's character on the television drama Dynasty, and his white Lab Harley after Heather Locklear's character on the short-lived TV series, LAX.*

*But the funniest story when it comes to naming pets is about the dogs my friend Jack's family had when he was growing up. The family dog was a yellow Lab named Cedric. When Cedric died and after a lengthy grieving period, Jack's Dad brought home another yellow Lab. The family couldn't agree on a name for their newest addition, so they named him Cedric 2. As years have passed, the family dogs are always referred to as Cedric 1 and Cedric 2.*

*Too bad the books with 6,000 dog names were not available then.*

# The Four-Legged Perspective

*"Dogs do speak, but only to those who know how to listen."*

—Orhan Pamuk

## The Parable of the Squirrel

I'm on my first walk of the morning, minding my own business, when I see his beady eyes, stumpy legs, and bushy tail spread out on my neighbor's stone wall. He acts like he doesn't see me, like he's not even there, like I'm not even here. He blends into the grayish-brown wall like an Alpo stain on a tan carpet.

He doesn't move, so I don't either. We lock eyes, each of us daring the other to make the first move. I leap toward him, forgetting Mary is attached. He jumps, or rather flies, to the closest tree and scatters to a high branch. I stand on my back paws, but still can't reach him. He makes a funny noise, like a Chihuahua in heat. He's obviously scared to come back down and face the Macster, Ruler of the Sidewalk, King of the Street, God of the Neighborhood.

I would have caught him if I didn't have Mary holding me down. I don't have time for this. I walk away with my head held high, leaving him crouched and lonely on a branch, muttering to no one.

🐾 🐾 🐾 🐾

*I've got to give Mac a lot of credit. I don't know if you call it a positive self-image, ignorance, or passion, but every time he sees a squirrel, he takes off after it with absolute surety that this time he'll catch his nemesis. If I don't see Rodent Rocky before he does, Mac practically pulls my arm out of its socket trying to intercept the ball of fur between the ground and seven feet into the tree.*

*The squirrel wins every time, and once out of Mac's reach, it looks down squeaking as if to say, "You stupid four-legged fatso. What makes you think you can catch me? Na na na na na." I picture the squirrel saying this as it moves its tiny, clawed hands back and forth behind its perky ears.*

*Mac never comes close to catching the squirrel, but he doesn't let it stop him from trying again. My determination in life pales in comparison to his persistence and confidence.*

*I give up the chase too easily. In business, I take "no" for an answer. Instead of picking up the phone again, or writing another email, or knocking on the door again, I let a single rejection set me back.*

*When it comes to dating, I wish I had Mac's conviction. He doesn't let 100 rejections stand in the way of going after the next eligible squirrel. Mac never worries others will say, "Who does she think she is? She'll never catch him."*

*On the flip side, what paradoxical squirrels am I chasing? Am I barking up the wrong tree thinking people will buy a book written by my dog?*

*Well, if you're reading this, then Mac probably caught the squirrel.*

## Neighbors in Training

Leashers are strange animals. They can pass each other on the street and act like the other one is not there. They don't look at each other, speak to one another, shake paws, smell each other's butt—nothing. It's an odd trait and a sad one, too. For the most part, leashers with dogs are friendlier and better adjusted than those without. The good news is that once a leasher gets a dog, change happens rather quickly. When a puppy is involved, it's even faster.

Take Mary, for example. She's a nice person; good teeth, fresh breath, smarter than the average human, but she didn't know many people in the neighborhood until I came along. I attracted lots of attention. Everyone stopped to admire my dreamy chocolate eyes peeping through eight pounds of vanilla fur. After admiring my cuteness for a few minutes, they started saying things like, "Ahhh, he still has puppy breath." Or "How old is he?" Or "What's his name?"

I insisted on lots of walks, and since Mary didn't like me peeing on the rug, we walked. "He sure is growing fast," neighbors would remark to Mary after stopping to pet me.

Eventually, after all the typical questions and the customary comments, conversations became more about them than about me. Soon Mary was talking to the neighbors without even mentioning my name. Human names were exchanged, and they began talking about leasher things, like the latest movie, the cute tenant who moved into The Colonial House, or the construction status of the new building.

Once leashers exchange names and genuine conversation, wonderful things begin to happen. Neighbors go to dinner together, give each other rides to the airport, get each other's mail, and check on each other during flu season. They become neighbors instead of mechanical bodies walking through the streets.

❧ ❧ ❧ ❧

*Although not recognized by Webster's, one definition for "dog" should be "four-legged social being who makes you talk to neighbors, whether you want to or not." Before Mac came into my life, I observed my neighbors through the tinted windows of my car. Canines' inherent gravitation toward each other's private parts changed that. As we dawdle, waiting for the round-robin sniffing to end, those of us on the other end of the leash are encouraged if not forced to speak to each other.*

*In time, you learn the names of your fellow dog lovers and conversing becomes something you want to do instead of have to do. You come to find out the green-haired guy with the four-pound Yorkshire terrier isn't as odd as he looks, unless you consider his career progression from an Anglican monk in the '60s to managing rock bands in the '80s unusual.*

*Other neighbors are not as colorful, literally or figuratively, but have become friends and confidants who are there for you on good days and bad. They excuse the way you look first thing in the morning and walk with you late at night, just to be safe.*

*However, this familiar relationship often requires Mac's presence. I've run into a neighbor at the mall or in the grocery store and, without Mac, I'm a stranger again. I speak their name and after moments of unreciprocated acknowledgement, I hear, "Oh, you're Mac's Mom."*

*I can think of no greater compliment.*

## Tails Don't Lie

You can always tell when I'm happy. My tail wags. I can't help it, and I don't want to. When I see Mary open the closet door, put on her shoes, grab her coat, take my leash off the hook, and tear off a blue plastic poop bag, I know we're going for a walk. I get so excited, and my tail wags. When Mary opens the kitchen closet, unscrews the lid from the large plastic drum that sits on the floor, and I hear the sweet sound of the plastic scoop dipping into the kibbles, I know it's time to eat. I am happy, and I wag my tail.

I've noticed the human version of wagging your tail is a smile. But a smile doesn't always mean a leasher is happy. Yesterday Mary was yelling at someone on the phone, and I heard them yelling back. When she hung up, I could see tears rolling down her cheeks. She crossed her arms on the desk in front of her, and laid her head down. I got up from my comfortable spot and laid beside her feet, hoping to comfort her. After a few minutes, she said, "Mac, let's get out of here. I need some fresh air."

As we started down the sidewalk, we ran into a neighbor who asked, "How are you today?" I wished he wouldn't have asked because I knew Mary was still upset, but she smiled and said, "Fine, thanks. And you?" Then when we got to the park and out of sight of other leashers, Mary started to cry again. I tried to cheer her up by wagging my tail extra fast. It didn't help much since I wasn't the one who made her cry. Maybe if she had been honest with the leasher on the street, he would have rubbed her belly to make her feel better and she would be happy now.

## New Ground

Yesterday Dillon, a large regal collie, and his leasher, Tad, took Mary and me for a long ride to a place I'd never been before. We went up and down lots of hills and around lots of turns. Finally we stopped and Tad opened the door. I jumped out of the car and landed on the ground like usual. But something was wrong with the ground. It was wet, but not the same wet as the sprinklers we avoid on our morning and evening walks. It was cold, which was good, because I'd rather be cold than hot.

But the ground didn't stay on the ground!

It rose up, covered my paws, four inches of my legs, and almost touched my wanker. I stood as still as a fire hydrant, letting the ground cling to my limbs.

I looked around to see that everything was white. The road was white, the plants were white, and the trees were white. There was even white stuff on the house we parked in front of. I was so distracted by this white attack that I forgot how much I had to pee. I wondered, "Can I pee on this white stuff?" Luckily I saw Dillon lift his leg and let her rip, so I did, too.

I turned around to see Tad and Mary scooping up the white ground in their hands and bunching it together. Then they threw the rounded ground at each other and called it *snowballs*. Well, you know I like the sound of that! Mary must have been reading my mind because she opened the back of the SUV and pulled out two tennis balls and a ball launcher named "Chuck-It."

Playing fetch in the snow was a weird experience. Mary would throw the ball. I'd see where it landed, but couldn't find it. When it left the launcher the ball was yellow, but when it landed, it turned white. Then I'd grab it in my mouth and the yellow would return. Running was hard because some of the places we played had tall snow. I would take a step, my feet would sink, and the thigh-high snow would tickle my belly. It was like getting a tummy bath and nothing else.

We had such fun playing in the snow. Mary and Tad laughed when one hit the other with a snowball. Even old Dillon, who's getting up there in years, played like a younger dog.

I like snow.

It's a magical blanket. Though cold on the outside, it keeps your insides warm.

## The Separation

### Day 1 – The Sneaky Getaway

Where did she go? Mary was behind me with Sammy Jo and one of her leashers. I bounded in the house expecting her to follow, but she was gone. I looked in all the usual places—the bathroom, the refrigerator, but no luck. Oh no. She's left me with them again.

The *them* I'm talking about is Sammy Jo, Jack, and Ron. Sammy Jo is a beautiful chocolate Lab with eyes sweet as liver. Her face is gray where it used to be brown. She walks slowly. She never runs but often looks like she wants to. The pads on her feet are worn out and she has to be careful where she steps. Ron has been Sammy Jo's leasher since she was little. He walks real slow so Sammy Jo doesn't have to hurry. Sammy Jo's second leasher, Jack, gives me extra treats when no one is looking.

It's not that I don't like staying with Sammy Jo and her leashers. I do. I just like it better when Mary is here, too. I wonder how long she'll be gone. I miss her. I miss my house. I miss my friends on the street. I think I'll curl up on the couch and sleep until Mary returns. It's a great couch. I'll save my energy so I can play ball with Mary when she gets home. There's not as many places to poop and pee as there are on my street, so I'll just go out when I absolutely have to.

I miss Mary. She didn't say her sappy goodbyes like usual. I wonder what that means. I hope she's not mad at me. I misbehaved a lot yesterday. I'll be a better dog when she returns.

### Day 2 – Adjusting

I like staying with Sammy Jo. Her toys still have the squeakers in them, or at least they did. There is a big bag full of treats Sammy Jo got for her birthday, so I get a different goodie every day. Because of our age and gender differences, we're not competitive.

I sleep late because I want to be rested when Mary comes home so we can go to the dog park, run up the canyon, play ball—all the things she likes to do.

### Day 3 – Settled In

Sammy Jo and I have grown used to this new (I hope temporary) arrangement. My Lab sister is a beautiful old gal. She just turned 13. I don't know how long she'll be here, so I need to spend as much time with her as I can.

Jack keeps taking pictures of me with his camera phone. He told me he was sending my picture to Mary because she misses me. Ahh, I miss her too. I wish I had a picture of her.

### Day 4 – Something's Up

The day started out like the other days since I last saw Mary, but by late afternoon, I could tell something was up. Ron got the red bag with my name on it out of the closet and put it on the couch. He picked up my toys and balls I'd left all over the house and under their two sofas. When we went outside, he took the red bag and put in it in the car before our walk. When we came back from peeing, we didn't go back in the house. We got in the car.

Whoopee! Sammy Jo and I were both excited to see where the car would take us!

Oh boy, oh boy, oh boy, I recognize that sign, that street, that building, that smell! I'm home! I'm standing in the back seat, rocking back and forth, ready to jump out as soon as the door opens. What is taking Ron so long to park the car? How hard can it be? Okay, we're parked. Open the door. Open the door. I don't need a leash, but Jack insists. Finally. I'm out of the car and pulling Jack up the sidewalk. I'm back where I'm supposed to be. Where's Mary? I can't wait to see her and hear, "Where's my booooyyyyyy?"

*I took the coward's way out and didn't go back into the house after our walk with Mac and Sammy Jo. I know Mac is in good, dog-loving hands while I'm visiting family in Virginia, but I don't want him to be trouble for friends who have graciously offered to dog-sit. Their 13-year-old Lab, Sammy Jo, is much less active. Mac is used to long walks and playing ball several times a day and will probably drive Jack and Ron crazy following them around from room to room, dropping a tennis ball at their feet, begging to go out. I give it a few days and call to see how Mac is doing. "How's my baby?"*

*"He's good," Jack responds.*

*"Is he driving you crazy?" Jack hesitates, and I think the worst. "What's wrong?"*

*"Mary, Mac's been sleeping ever since you left. He moves from one couch to the other, to the chair, and back to the sofa."*

*I'm stunned. "Are you serious? Did you drug him?" Jack laughs and puts Ron on the phone to confirm Mac's slug-like demeanor. "He's been off the sofa to eat and go to the bathroom, but that's about it."*

*Jack and Ron take turns sending hourly pictures of Mac in the same position, curled up in a ball on the end of the sofa.*

*Why the personality change? Am I an easy target who jumps every time he barks? Is he depressed? Is this his time to relax and rejuvenate and return to me with more energy than ever? Maybe it's his way of saying I'm the most important person in his life, and without me, he's nothing.*

*Suffice it to say, I think my dog is co-dependent.*

## Moving On Up

This morning, my friend Arrow and his leashers drove by and waved. Arrow was sitting in the front seat. Not the back seat, not the cargo area, but the front seat! His boy leasher was driving, and his girl leasher was sitting in the back. At first I was jealous. But then I thought, "Good for him. If he can do it, so can I!"

So this afternoon, when Mary lifted the hatch for me to get in our SUV, I sat on the cold floor of the garage, staring at her. "Get in," she said. I looked at her. Why should I sit in the cargo area when there's a perfectly good back seat no one uses? The back window doesn't open, so I never get to feel the wind in my face. And, it smells like a dog back there. "Up here," she pleaded as she patted her hand on the rough cargo carpet. This time I moved. But I didn't jump into the back. No, I quietly strolled toward the front of the car and sat beside the backseat door. I didn't want to push my luck demanding to sit up front. I sat confidently, like I deserved more than a place you put groceries.

Finally, Mary sighed. She moved my blanket and beach towel from the far back to the back seat, where I will forever ride. As we drove around, I beamed with joy at my accomplishment. Thanks, Arrow. You're my Rosa Parks. Yes, I watch the History channel too.

*Today when I opened the back hatch for Mac to jump into the car, he just sat on the garage floor. "Get in," I said as I patted the upholstered floor of the cargo area. "Up here." He stared at me with a nervous look on his face. I felt so bad. Last week I shut the hatch too fast and caught his tail in the door. He howled loudly and tragically, and I felt the psychological anguish of his physical pain. I apologized and kissed him profusely but it seems now*

*I've scarred him for life. He's jumped into the back of my SUV hundreds of times without incident, but this one horrible time is what he remembers.*

*My guilt mounted. I patted the floor of the cargo area again, "Come on up. I promise I won't shut the door on your tail." He was having none of this. He walked around to the passenger door and sat there staring at it, as if to say, "Please don't hurt me. I'm begging you. Don't make me ride back there ever again."*

*I picked up the blanket and beach towel that covered the floor of the cargo area and moved it to the back seat. Mac jumped in quickly without being asked. I could see him in my rearview mirror as I started the car. There was a look of relief on his face. At every stoplight, I reached back and scratched him under his chin or behind his ears, or rubbed my index finger on the bridge of his nose. He smiled at me as if to say, "I forgive you."*

## Rainbow Fur

Mary and I live on a colorful street. The grass is green and so is Boots' leasher's hair. The sky is blue and so is Viking's leasher's hair. I've never seen a dog with green or blue fur. I did see a dog with pink fur at Starbucks one day. She had pink hair, a pink dress, and pink nails. So did her leasher. Our town has all the colors of the rainbow. And there are lots of rainbows around our town.

This was a big issue the last time leashers went to their polls to do something called *voting*. Some leashers didn't want girl leashers to be a family with other girl leashers, or boy leashers to be a family with other boy leashers.

I don't like leashers or dogs based on whether they are a boy or a girl. I rely on my sense of smell. I can smell whether a leasher or a dog is kind or aggressive. I think leashers would be happier if they met, smelled each other, and then decided whether to walk down the street together, share a bone, or just growl and walk away.

# Special Times and Special Leashers

*"Love is a four-legged word."*

—Bumper sticker

## Houseguest

Mary opened the door and with her was a leasher I'd never seen before. The leasher was shorter than most with a white fur top, wrinkled ankles, and spots on her feet. She moved slowly. She held tightly to the handrail and put both feet on the same step before moving to the next one.

When she talked, she sounded like Mary. Mary called her *Mom*. She smelled like Fig Newtons and medicated lotion. I barked loudly, and she backed away from me. I barked louder. She was afraid of me, and I felt powerful. Mom unzipped one of the bags Mary had carried in from the car and pulled out a bone, which I quickly took off her hands. Okay, maybe she's not so bad after all. She looked at me while I was eating. I barked again, and she looked away. Mary told me to stop.

I could sense my liking Mom was important to Mary, so I eased up on the barking and started working on the liking.

After a few days, I realized Mom was not much trouble and didn't get in my way or come between Mary and me. I still got to sleep in Mary's bed, play ball, and go to the park. We took Mom to the beach, but she stayed in one spot instead of walking and playing ball with us.

At night, Mom sat on the sofa with her eyes closed and head down. Growling sounds came out of her little lips. When a growl was particularly loud, she popped her head up and looked from side to side to see where the sound came from. A few minutes later, she'd drop her head again and start growling some more.

Mary slowed down the pace of her life so Mom could keep up. She took good care of Mom like she does with me. When Mom wanted something from the refrigerator, Mary got it for her. When Mom went to bed at night, Mary helped her up the stairs. When Mom watched *Wheel of Fortune*, Mary watched it, too.

Just when I was getting used to the slow little leasher, Mary came home without her. Our lives returned to normal. But while Mom was here, I saw a different side of Mary. As with most of the others, I like that side.

## I'm Such a Blessing

Mary took me in the car to somewhere I've never smelled before. We were in the back yard of someone's house. It was the biggest house I'd ever seen. It had a tower at the top with a tall point. Someone important must live here. Perhaps it's a famous musician because I heard pretty music and bells ringing from a window in the tower. Two big front doors opened and lots of leashers headed our way. Some of the leashers had dogs, some had cats, and some had cages with birds and furry things that looked like rats but prettier.

Normally I would have been chasing the cats, rats, and birds, but there was something about this place that took away my urge to chase. Besides, the wires in their cages were too small to stick my paws into. I sniffed a few of the other dogs, who all agreed we had no idea what was going on.

A lady leasher in a long black dress holding a book seemed to be in charge. She told everyone to put their heads down while she read from her book. After reading words I didn't understand and something about *A Men*, she started bossing everyone around. She told the leashers with dogs to stand in line on one side of her and the leashers with the non-dogs to stand on the other side.

Mary and I waited our turn behind a leasher with a Great Dane, two girls with little white dogs who wouldn't shut up, and an older man with a cane and a Lab mix. I wasn't sure what was happening, but everyone was smiling and hurrying to get in the line, so I did, too, thinking the leasher in black was handing out treats. I was wrong.

When Mary and I got to the front of the line, the leasher poured something wet in her hand, placed her hand on my head and said, "Dear Lord, bless Mac and always keep him in your care. Bless Mary. May Mac continue to give her joy and love and her to him in return." We moved on and the leasher in black was on to her next victim.

What? I don't understand. That's it? No bacon, no pizza, no treats, not even a kibble, just something wet on my head? I looked around. There was nothing to eat, but I admit I did feel special. Like a big dog in the sky had whispered to me, "You are a good dog and I love you." Maybe if I listen harder he'll tell me where the leasher in the long black dress keeps her food.

*I read in the bulletin that there would be a "Blessing of the Animals" in the church courtyard after a Sunday service. I was new to Hollywood United Methodist and this was another way in which it differed from the more conservative Methodist church I attended as a child in Virginia. I was intrigued and thought maybe a blessing from God could reduce Mac's shedding—probably not the church's intent. I noticed some congregants bring their dogs to church each Sunday, but I thought it best to ease Mac into Christianity by first bringing him to the blessing ceremony.*

*The blessing was held in the church's courtyard after the 11:00 a.m. service. After a brief prayer, Pastor Karen asked the congregants and their pets to form two lines. Since Pastor Karen was allergic to cats and leery of snakes and gerbils, she directed those of us with dogs to line up in front of her and the non-canines to form a line in front of Reverend Dean.*

*When we got to the front of the dog line, the pastor dipped her hand in holy water, placed it on Mac's head and her dry hand on my shoulder, while reciting "Dear Lord, bless Mac and always keep him in your care. Bless Mary. May Mac continue to give her joy and love and her to him in return."*

*The brief ritual the pastor performed seemed to have a lasting effect on Mac as we walked in silence to the car. The simple prayer carried us through the rest of the day and into the evening.*

*As he jumped onto my bed that night, I thought to myself, "I don't know how I ever lived without him or what I'll do when he's gone. But for now, I'm enjoying the blessing of my officially blessed dog."*

## Runyon Heaven

*A popular haunt for dog owners in Los Angeles is Runyon Canyon, one of the few open spaces in the city where you can legally hike with your dog off leash. From dawn to dusk, dogs and their owners come outfitted with poop bags and water bottles to hike one of half-a-dozen trails. The vertical climb keeps Mac exhausted until the next day. He makes the experience harder than need be by running in and out and up and down the canyon rather than staying on the path, which is plenty difficult for me.*

*Mac and I get separated, but I see him resting under one of the few shade trees. I'm grateful for an excuse to rest my calves and replenish my lung capacity. Not enough minutes pass before Mac drops the ball at my feet signaling it's time to resume our hike.*

*My huffing, puffing, and sweating are worth every breath once I arrive at the top and gaze upon the city of Los Angeles below. Mac and I split a bottle of water before I climb onto a tall wooden bench where my feet never touch the ground. Mac stretches out under the bench and enjoys the shade from my butt covering more of the bench's wooden slats than I'd like.*

*I have a 360-degree view of Los Angeles and the San Fernando Valley. At this distance, traffic, horns, and city noise are on mute. When it's clear, I can see Catalina Island peering over the Pacific like a protective partner.*

*Runyon is a spiritual place, a virtual church with no steeples or stained glass. Communion is a half-drunk bottle of Aquafina. Runners panting and dogs barking are the choir. I scan the city below and pray for family and friends, for the wheelchair-bound man in front of Starbucks on Hollywood Boulevard, and for the family of the murdered teen whose coverage consumed the morning news.*

*I'd like to stay longer but the day calls. I hop down from the bench and Mac and I head down the mountain to cross off the less-spiritual things on our daily to-do list.*

❧ ❧ ❧ ❧

Today Mary and I went to Runyon Canyon. Runyon, as we locals call it, is Heaven on Earth. We enter the metal gates, Mary removes my leash, and it's party time. I run up to a German shepherd who smells like soap and cereal. While I'm checking out the shepherd, a skinny gray Schnauzer sticks its nose in my behind. We run around in circles until I decide to break away and study the underside of a big black Newfoundland. Mary catches up to me, opens her backpack, and pulls out a tennis ball. Now she has my attention. She throws the ball, and I take off running.

A trip to Runyon has two parts, the up part and the down part. The up part is hot and hard. My legs get tired and my mouth gets dry because I'm chasing the ball uphill. If I don't get to it quick enough, the ball falls down the canyon. I dive into tall dry grasses and sticky bushes, but can't find my ball. Instead I grab a ball someone else lost and drag myself and the ball up the steep hill. I've got stickers in my fur and dirt in my mouth. I'm panting hard. I rest under a big shade tree. I'm hot and tired, but boy am I having fun! Mary catches up to me, and we continue to climb the mountain together. Mary throws the ball, but I'm tired, so I wait for it to roll down to me. I keep it in my mouth for the rest of the up part.

Finally, we reach the top where I get to rest under a long bench to catch my breath. Mary pours water into a bowl and I lap it up and wait for more. She climbs onto the bench I'm lying under. I peep up between the wooden slats of the bench. Mary's eyes are closed like she's asleep, but I know she's not. She has a peaceful, happy look on her face like the one I have when I take a break from playing ball and rest in the grass that tickles my tummy. Mary looks the same way, except I think her tummy is being tickled from the inside. She opens her eyes and stares down at the city we came from. It's a loud and busy place when you're in it, but there's no sound when you're above it, resting under a bench in Runyon.

After we get our breath back, Mary jumps off the bench. I get up, and we begin the hike down the hill. The down part of the trip is much faster than the up part. At the bottom of the canyon, I roll in a mud puddle underneath the drinking spout. Mary doesn't care that this will get her car dirty, because she sees how good it makes me feel. Mary puts me back on a leash and we leave Runyon's gates, tired on the outside but awake on the inside.

## My First Thanksgiving

I was eight months old when I had my first Thanksgiving, and I thought it might be my last. Mary got up early and stayed in the kitchen for a long time working her way from the refrigerator to the sink, to the counter, to the dishwasher, to the stove, and back again. She washed, chopped, stirred, and cooked. Midway through this unfamiliar routine, the kitchen started smelling good. I hung out at her feet to catch falling macaroni and boiled egg whites. After what seemed like forever, she put the good-smelling stuff in big dishes, covered them with shiny paper, and packed them in the car.

We spent what was left of the morning and part of the afternoon in Hank and Ruby Belle's yard. Hank is a mixer, part German shepherd and part something else. Ruby Belle is a Bloodhound whose layers of skin make it look like her face is falling.

I was having fun playing with the big dogs, doing everything they did. If they drank from the gutter, so did I. If they barked at the fence, I did too. If they rolled in the dirt, I was there. I was trying so hard to keep up that I didn't realize all the leashers had gone into the house without us.

I stood on my hind legs with my front paws on the back door, trying to get Mary's attention. I could hear her laughing and making noise in the kitchen, but she never looked my way. I whined, hoping Mary would let me in, but did so quietly so Hank and Ruby Belle wouldn't think I was a cry doggy. I eventually gave up and laid down in the yard.

After a quick nap, I heard the back door creak open. A leasher walked out. This was my chance to sneak in the house and find Mary. But I wasn't the only one who heard the door. Hank and Ruby Belle charged toward the leasher. We got to his legs at the same time. Surprised by our twelve legs at his feet, he pushed us away. Ruby Belle fell on Hank, who fell on my leg, and then it happened.

Great God of Tennis Ball Poop Trees Birds Oh Mamma Treats, it hurt so bad! I cried in pain. The door opened and the once cheerful leashers ran to my side. Rex, Hank, and Ruby Belle's leasher told everyone to stand back. Mary was crying. I didn't want her to cry; I wanted her to make my leg stop hurting.

Every time Rex touched me, it hurt more. I flung my legs, my head, all of my body up and down and side to side to make the pain go away. It wouldn't. I knew they wanted to help me, but didn't they understand how much it hurt? The next time Rex tried to grab my leg, I used my teeth to stop him. That's when he put a cup with a strap over my mouth. It made me feel helpless. I couldn't cry as loud. But the pain was still loud.

Rex picked me up and took me to the car. Mary sat in the back seat rubbing my ears and telling me it would be okay. Rex drove us to the vet's office where they put a needle in my thigh. I got sleepy.

I don't remember much about the next few days. Each time I'd start to remember the pain, I'd cry, and Mary put a pill in my mouth.

I liked the pills. When I took them, I smelled butcher shops with bones stacked to the ceiling for me to taste, felt Mary rubbing my tummy so long that I had to tell her to stop, and saw red, green, blue and yellow tennis balls with leashers who loved to throw them.

But then the pills stopped and so did the vision of bones, belly rubs, and balls. I was left with a hard white thing on my leg. Mary called it a *cast*, short for *catastrophe*.

I tried to run and play, but it hurt to do the things I like to do. Mary stayed by my side with sadness and guilt in her eyes. It wasn't her fault, but I played along to get ice cream and extra treats.

The news of my cast spread throughout the neighborhood. Everyone wanted to know what happened. I got lots of attention and "Aahs." After a while, I forgot the cast was on my leg. I ran, chased balls, and smelled poop, all the things I'd done pre-cast.

One day I got bored and ate my cast while Mary was gone. She was really mad. I thought she was going to break my other legs. After I'd eaten the third cast, Mary put a lamp shade on me. This is known as the "cone of shame." Since I wasn't able to eat my cast anymore, my leg healed. I was back to perfect except for the funny way my once-broken leg sticks out when I sit or run.

So every November, along with giving thanks for Mary, trees, the ocean, balls, and poop, I also give thanks for the things I haven't had since my first Thanksgiving: gravel, pain, pills, muzzles, casts, and lamp shades.

*I will never forget the sound of Mac's pain reverberating in my ears and in my heart that Thanksgiving Day. I was washing dishes when I heard it. I ran outside to see my eight-month-old puppy screaming in pain. Mac's cries were piercing and his body was writhing from side to side. Rex got to him first and was holding him tight to his chest.*

*"I think his leg is out of socket. Do you want me to try to put it back in place or do you want to go to the vet?"*

*Tears were streaming down my face as I struggled to make a decision. "Let's go to the vet." Rex had a muzzle from being a dog owner for life and put it on Mac, which only reduced the painful shrieking to a more intense, painful whimper.*

*Rex drove and I held Mac in my lap. I've often envisioned the perfect way to get out of doing dishes after the Thanksgiving meal, and this wasn't it. The 24-hour vet was only a few miles away. They sedated Mac right away and sent him to get an X-ray. After I signed a tear-stained form agreeing to their estimated fee of $500, the girl at the front desk told me it was no use waiting. I could call back in an hour or so for the diagnosis.*

*I left feeling like the worst mother in the world. An hour later, I called the vet and they informed me Mac had a fracture. They referred me to a surgeon at a surgery center that was closed until the following day. I could either come get him now or pick him up in the morning on the way to the surgeon.*

*As much as I wanted to hold him in my arms, bury my nose in his neck, and tell him I was sorry, I decided it was better not to move him. I went home to an empty house with an answering machine full of messages from concerned friends that I didn't have the energy to return.*

*On the way out of my garage the next morning, I ran into my neighbor George who, after his third cup of coffee, was ready to discuss the previous day's holiday feast. When he saw my tears and heard my story, he said he was going with me. In hindsight, I'm not sure what I would have done without George. In sad times, when decisions have to be made, the sting of being alone is so powerful.*

*George picked up a groggy Mac and put him in the car while I signed his release papers. I drove to the surgery center with one eye on the road and the other on the bundle of fur in George's lap. The surgery center took us right away and within half an hour, we were sitting with the surgeon in a sterile cramped room.*

*Dr. Canter gave us two options for treating Mac's broken leg. She could either operate for $4,000 or put a cast on it for $800. I asked the doctor what she would do if it were her dog. She answered, "Well, I would operate, but I wouldn't be paying $4,000. Mac is young and the break is clean. Unless you plan to show him, the cast will work fine."*

*I didn't know what to do. Fortunately, George was there to help me reconcile my decision with my bank account.*

*A casted Mac was the toast of the neighborhood. All the dogs gathered round for a sniff, their version of signing his cast. He was groggy at first, but after the pain pills and antibiotics were no longer needed, he was back to his old self, running and playing ball, except now he had a new chew toy. He chewed off two casts before Dr. Canter threatened to charge me again. That's when the lamp shade came out, guilt or no guilt. Mac tried to play the pity party card, but I stayed strong until his leg healed.*

*After eight weeks, the cast, pills and lamp shade were gone. The only physical reminder of Mac's first Thanksgiving is a back left leg that juts out from the side of his hefty body when he sits, like an unhinged oar dangling from a rowboat.*

*The deeper scars are in me. The piercing shrieks from a little puppy that just wanted to be with me echo in my mind as I recall the day. I haven't heard anything like it since, and I pray I never will.*

## Picture Perfect

Today, Mary is taking a picture for our Christmas card that she sends to leashers I haven't even sniffed. I enjoy this annual event because there are good treats and lots of 'em. When Mary tells me to look one way or stand another, I ignore her. So I get more treats.

Treats aren't the only way to get my focus. Mary pulls a new, yellow, never-been-chased tennis ball out of her bag of tricks.

"Sit," Mary tells me, followed by more commands to stay, lie down, speak, and so on, while she holds the tennis ball above the camera. I give her my best cute-dog pose and she takes a picture.

"Down."

I obey while keeping my eyes on the ball. She moves the ball to the right. I move my head to follow it. She moves the ball to the left, and I look that way. I'm over this game so I lunge for the fuzzy Penn 3, but she lifts the ball above her head out of my reach and yells.

"Stay!"

I know it's no use to fight her on this. Experience tells me I'm not getting the ball until she gets the perfect picture.

*It begins after Thanksgiving, slowly at first, but picking up speed by mid-December. Crammed in my small mailbox amongst the multitude of catalogs are Christmas cards, letters, and pictures of friends and family.*

*Holiday cards are reciprocal. During the five-year span I let the business of the season engulf me, I crossed this custom off my December to-do list. After a few years, my Santa bucket full of cards dwindled to a small stack. When I started sending cards again, my card receiving resumed. I owe the reinstatement of this lovely tradition to Mac.*

*I love pictures, as evidenced by the 24 photo albums under my bed.*

*Albums 1-20 chronologically represent my life from baby pictures to the time before digital pictures, somewhere around 2005.*

*Albums A-D contain pictures taken in more formal settings, often by professionals. These include school pictures, wedding pictures and pictures received in holiday cards and pictures that are themselves the cards.*

*Holiday pictures chronicle a cute four-year-old becoming a gawky 10-year-old; the cute boy in the Little League uniform whose oversized pants now hang low on his hips; and the family posed in coordinating holiday outfits in front of a new house significantly larger than the one in last year's card. Enclosed holiday letters describe in detail the daily itinerary of a family's two-week vacation with casual mention of their perfect children's athletic prowess and straight A's.*

*Before Mac, I didn't see the point or didn't have the confidence to include a picture of myself in my Christmas cards. While I don't have the big house or a 15-year-old child with a scholarship to Yale, my annual "Mac and me" holiday card is a way to share a part of me that for years stayed quiet.*

## Camp Christmas

*When I leave town for the holidays, Mac goes to camp. What I call "camp" is five acres of land in Acton, California, about an hour's drive from Los Angeles in steady traffic. For a week, Mac lives in a 3,000-square-foot dorm with others dogs, each with a private six-by-twelve-foot room with their own bed and blanket. The camp proprietor is Donna, a long, lanky forty-something tomboy with no makeup and long dark hair with streaks of gray. Her life is devoted to dogs, those she owns and those she cares for when their owners are away. Donna picks up and returns her four-legged guests in a custom air-conditioned van; rows of seats have been replaced by rows of wire crates two high.*

*I've never been to Acton, but I am comfortable sending Mac there sight unseen. Donna loves dogs, and Mac loves her. When Donna arrives, she loops a rope around his neck, and he willingly goes with her to the van and gets into the wire crate. He normally hates crates. He doesn't even say goodbye. I want him to be happy, but strangely it hurts my feelings. It's a chink in the pedestal I thought he'd placed me on.*

*Once he's in the van and on his way, I pack for my trip. Mac gets quiet and allusive when I pull out a suitcase, so it's easier on both of us if I wait.*

*While I'm in Virginia with my family for the Christmas holidays, I miss Mac but don't worry about him. I know he is with someone, be it dog or person, twenty-four hours a day. I know he gets a lot of exercise. I know he gets to be a dog. But I miss him.*

*I schedule Mac's return for the day after mine. At the start of the two-hour drop-off window, I get anxious and can't concentrate on my work. I peek through the drapes every time I hear a loud engine outside.*

*Finally I see Donna's van in the driveway. I run out the door before she gets to mine. She's let Mac out of the cage and has a rope around his neck. He sees me and runs like a thoroughbred to greet me, pulling Donna along behind him.*

*"You can let him go," I tell her before he pulls her arm out of its socket.*

*"Oh, I missed you so much. I missed you so much," I coo as I rub my hands through the fur under his chin and bury my nose behind his ear. He moves his paws back and forth in place and his body wiggles like an out-of-control Slinky. He runs between Donna and me, not quite knowing who to stay with.*

*Donna bids farewell and hops back in the van to deliver other holiday guests to their homes. I wrap my arms around Mac, pull him to my chest, and tell him again how much I've missed him. Like an embarrassed teenager trying to prove his independence, he struggles to get away. I hold him tighter. For an instant, I wonder if he wishes he were still with Donna at the ranch. Seemingly reading my mind, Mac stills his body, tilts his head, stares me in the eyes, and gives me a big wet kiss.*

*Mac is home, and all is right with the world.*

Not long after the Christmas card photo shoot, it happens. Mary gets my red bag with the letter "M" on it out of the closet. She puts kibbles and treats in plastic bags and puts those bags in my "M" bag. She sits the bag on the chair by the door. She hugs me longer and more than usual. I get nervous and crawl under the table to avoid her clutching.

A big van pulls into the driveway. Donna the driver comes to our door with treats in one hand and a rope in the other. Donna has long black-and-white hair. She smells more like a dog than a leasher. She puts the rope around my neck and leads me to her van, where my cage awaits. Mary stands on the sidewalk with her hands in her pockets offering no assistance. She won't look me in the eye. I can't tell if she wants me to stay or go. I don't think she knows herself.

"Come on Mackie, it's for your own good," says Donna as she pats the bottom of a wire cage.

She wins because she has a rope around my neck. There are other dogs in their own temporary jails who don't like it any more than I do. I check them out, and then the door closes. I would have liked one last look at Mary. I would have liked to have said goodbye.

We ride and ride and ride. Finally, we get to Donna's ranch. I am at camp, and I love it here. We're let out of jail one-by-one into a big field that is green in the summer and brown in the winter. We run to our favorite bush or fence post. There is room to run around and lots of dogs to play with. Depending on how many dogs are at the ranch, I may or may not get my own room. I don't mind sharing because all we do is sleep there.

Dogs are not the only guests at Donna's ranch. There are squirrels and possums and coyotes, but we've been told to stay away from the coyotes because they're mean and run in gangs. A fence divides us from a field of cows, donkeys, pigs, and goats. We smell each other through the triangle holes in the metal barrier.

Donna keeps a strict schedule. At sunrise she opens my bedroom door and lets me play in the yard. I wish Mary had a yard. I get to pee and poop and run around without a leash around my neck. It's very freeing. While we're playing, Donna calls us one-by-one into the dining room for breakfast. I eat quickly so I can go back out to play.

After breakfast and free time, Donna takes off in her mobile jail while I take a nap in my room. I sleep soundly until I hear Donna's van coming up the long gravel driveway. I look out my bedroom window to see more campers getting out of the van.

There's a dog who looks like me. I wonder if we're related. Some look scared like I did my first time here. I remind myself to be extra friendly to the newcomers. Donna plays ball with us until it's time to eat again. After supper, we play outside until bedtime.

Time passes quickly at camp. I feel like I just got here when one morning Donna calls me into her office after breakfast. Her helper gives me a bath, clips my toenails, and cleans my ears. I've learned that this is my signal that I get to see Mary today.

I get a funny feeling in my belly. I want to see Mary, but I don't want to leave the ranch. Donna puts me in a cage in the van. I'm exhausted from my bath, and I sleep all the way home. I wake up when the van stops in front of my house. Mary is there to greet me. I wag my tail and run to her with sleepy eyes. Then I run back to Donna to thank her for my time at the ranch. I'm half asleep and can't remember who I ran to last, so I keep running back and forth.

Now it's time to be happy to see Mary and sad to see Donna go. Why can't everyone we love stay in the same place?

## Happy Birthday Sammy Jo

Yesterday was Sammy Jo's fourteenth birthday party.

There were lots of leashers and dogs, probably twenty of us and thirty of them. There was food for leashers and food for dogs.

I enjoyed both.

The leashers put pointed cardboard hats on our heads. I tried to take mine off with my right paw but there was a string under my chin that wouldn't let me. The hat was stupid and uncomfortable. But I decided not to let such an insignificant thing ruin my party—I mean *Sammy Jo's* party.

Leashers brought presents for the birthday gal. They were wrapped in pretty paper and bows, but I could smell that many of them contained treats. Ron put a crown on Sammy Jo's head and wrapped a string of purple feathers around her neck. There was loud music. The leashers were loud, too. I couldn't hear myself pant.

Through all the chaos, Sammy Jo and I had a moment. I caught her staring at me out of the corner of my eye as I was prying the paper off my third ice-cream cup. Her eyes left mine and turned to watch the activity surrounding her. There was a smile on her face. She was taking it all in, loving it all, especially her two leashers.

The look on her face said so much.

She was a matriarch looking out over her family, thinking about her long and happy life, knowing this would be her last birthday in the park. She saw me looking at her and gave me the silent sign to keep this between the two of us.

I granted her request and went back to my ice cream.

*Yesterday was Sammy Jo's birthday party. Ron and Jack's annual soirée has become the canine event of the season. This year about 30 humans and as many dogs showed up to celebrate the chocolate Lab's fourteenth birthday in West Hollywood Park. There were hot dogs and hamburgers and all the fixings for the humans and for the dogs, beautifully decorated Sprinkles cupcakes from the famous Beverly Hills bakery, along with doggy ice cream cups.*

*Begrudgingly, people and dogs alike were forced to wear pointed birthday hats, the kind with the elastic string that pinches the fat under your chin. Only Sammy Jo was exempt from a cardboard head cone. A rhinestone encrusted tiara sat lopsided on her head as a purple feather boa encircled her neck and flowed softly over her upper torso. The guest of honor looked like a misplaced princess, lying elegantly beside the slightly dented chrome trashcan.*

*You could see her body moving slowly as she lay, breathing heavily from a more active day than she was used to. But she never stopped smiling. In years past, she would wind in and out of guests' legs, looking for crumbs amongst the wrapping paper and balloons. This year, she was content to watch her guests enjoy the afternoon. It was a fun day for humans and animals—laughter, barking, eating, and conversation.*

*Amongst the people and the dogs, there was never any mention of the elephant in the park. This was probably Sammy's Jo's last birthday.*

## Mommy Jr.

Laura lived with Mary and me when I was a puppy. Mary called her a "roommate". I called her Mommy Jr. For the first year of my life, Mary went away every day, so I thought Laura was my leasher. I learned a lot from her.

She taught me to speak. Leashers think this is funny since Laura speaks a lot. And I mean a *lot*. She talks loud and fast. I crawl under the table in front of the sofa to get away from the noise. The table is low to the ground so her voice doesn't sound so loud.

Laura was strict but I loved her for it. It made me a better dog.

She used bacon to make me do what she wanted. She likes bacon. That's a passion we share.

"Sit. Stay," she said firmly. Then she put a piece of crispy bacon in my bowl. It smelled so good. I ran to the bowl as fast as I could to grab the delicious strip.

But Laura bacon-blocked me. She held her hand up and said, "Stay." I sat back down and stayed for what seemed like forever. I couldn't take it anymore, so I ran toward the bowl.

"Ah, ah, ah, I didn't say 'alright'," Laura sing-songed and picked up my bowl. This went on for days before I finally caved in and waited for her to say the magic word. I realized that was the only way I was going to get my bacon.

Mommy Jr. knew how important a full tummy is to me. "Got milk? Got milk? Got milk?" she said. I got so excited my paws left the floor getting to the kitchen. I stood by the refrigerator with my tail wagging, waiting for her to take out the carton. I followed her to my bowl, panting with excitement as she poured the sweet white liquid.

She made eating fun. She made everything fun.

Then one day, Laura moved out of our house, and we became a one-leasher home.

I miss Mommy Jr. She still comes to see me. Sometimes she spends the night on the sofa. I love those nights because it reminds me of when I was a puppy, when we were all together. But spending the night is not the same as living together. It's not the same as having her here to lick every morning and playing "Got milk?" every night.

And I sure do miss that bacon.

# Women are from Venus... Dogs aren't

*"Mac's needs are simple. He doesn't need a closet full of clothes or an iPod full of songs. He has one coat and doesn't mind if it gets dirty. His music is a squirrel rustling in a tree and rain water rolling down the street."*

—Mary

## The Best Places to Eat

I love to eat. I love to eat what I'm supposed to and what I'm not supposed to. This is one of the reasons I like to go outside. When we're inside, Mary has control of what I eat. Outside is a different story.

Sometimes I pretend I have to pee so I can cruise the street for something to eat. I have the best luck right in the crack where the tar meets the sidewalk. That's where thin sheets of paper with Mexican food and greasy McDonald's bags hide. I check the tires of parked cars to see if they have food smashed in them. I also like the dumpster where people with bad aim throw food away. The dumpster misses are hard to get because Mary jerks my leash when I get close.

Today on our walk, I smell a jackpot. I look around and there it is, a bag, peeking out from behind the right rear tire on the blue car parked too close to the curb. It's stuck between the rubber and the cement. If I can just get my paw in there and pull gently before Mary yanks me back. Ahh, it's a fresh one! It's probably left over from today's lunch, breakfast at the latest. No, definitely lunch because the smell is distinctly hamburger and French fries as opposed to Egg McMuffin and hash browns. From the outside of the greasy bag, you can't tell the difference. The potato smells are similar except the French fries have a stronger scent, usually because the previous eater left a fry or two for me. Hash browns rarely get left behind. The Egg McMuffin has cleaner grease than a Big Mac. Visions of both spuds dance in my head as I'm able to tug the bag out of the tire's grip without Mary seeing me.

I move too quickly, and she hears the bag crumble. She pulls me away. I place my right paw on top of the paper sack, and it scoots with me as I resist her pull. In the end, Mary wins, and I snort in disgust at double losses. Not only have I failed to get what's inside the bag, but

I've left it out in the open for Homer or Dillon to effortlessly scoop up what should have been mine.

Life sucks sometimes.

*Mac is a pig, constantly rooting the ground for food as we walk the neighborhood. One of his favorite "restaurants" is the treads of tires parked on the street, where he searches for a car whose primary purpose is to drive back and forth over anything edible. He considers each tread to be his personal vending machine. A9 for leftover McDonald's, B2 for Taco Bell, and C6 for Subway. He favors the crevice where the cement curb meets the pavement, where food accidentally falls as the black rubber vending machines are being refilled.*

*After he checks out the street vendors, he dives headfirst into a row of three-feet-high sword ferns. I smile at the wagging tail of his headless body as he scours the bushes for the treasure his keen sense of smell has led him to. He emerges with a dirty face, leaves on his head, and the thick crust of a half-eaten pizza in his mouth.*

*But not all his meals are happenstance. Mac's charm has endeared him to the valets at the tony Mondrian Hotel on Sunset Boulevard, where the men and women in khaki pants and crisp white shirts often share a portion of their breakfast burrito or Starbucks bagel with Mac. Further east as we near our street, Mac makes his way to Gus, the dog-loving valet at The Standard, who usually keeps a dog treat or two in his pocket.*

*Whether it's the hunter or the charmer in him, Mac has found a way to make each morning a walking brunch.*

## Language Barriers

There are advantages to not speaking the same language. At night, when I know Mary wants to go in, I keep strolling and sniffing. I don't have to go "doggy business," but Mary doesn't know that. She tells me to do my business, but she can't understand that I don't have to. Every once in a while I poop on the living room rug so she doesn't assume I can wait until morning.

Another advantage is you get to act like you don't know what she's talking about. I know I'm not supposed to lay on the red sofa in the living room or in the big square chair in the bedroom, but I get away with it because of our language barrier.

Now there are definitely some disadvantages to not being able to talk. Like the time she brought home the huge bag of something called *turducken*. Give me turkey or give me duck, but don't give me turducken. Of course, I ate it. I eat everything. It made my tummy sick, which turned into runny doggy business and a few accidents on the rug before she finally got a clue and switched back to good ol' chicken.

It's also hard to get through to her that I like to go with her whenever she leaves the house. But if I have to wait in the car for hours, I'd just as soon be home watching television. I never know when the car door opens if I'm in for a trip to the dog park or a boring hour of watching people put groceries in their cars.

But there is a language that doesn't require understanding words, whimpers, or barks. At night when I curl up beside her and she scratches my tummy, we're both saying "I love you" in our own special way.

## Bad Mood

"Mac, you're my best friend," she whines as she reaches down and wraps her arms around my body while I stand patiently at the gate waiting to get to the street. You know what Mary, maybe I don't want to be your best friend. Maybe I don't want the responsibility of keeping you happy and from being alone. It's a lot of pressure that I don't need right now. You've been yanking my chain all day. This morning, all I wanted to do was pee on the new bush where the Mastiff went so I could show him who's boss on this street. But you made me go where no one else had gone. What fun is that? When we were playing ball, if I returned the ball *slightly* out of your reach, you sat there and said, "Closer." I had to run back and drop it by your feet because you wouldn't get off your fanny. When you *finally* put some food in my bowl, you held your hand up and made me wait 10 seconds before I could eat. What's all that about? And while I'm throwing one of my rare temper tantrums, why did you have to cut my balls off? Is that any way to treat a "best friend"?

*When we go out for a walk, there is a gate I must open to get from the walkway by my condo to the street. Mac stands patiently at the gate waiting to run out to pee, to see his friends, to see what scents await him in his world. When he's standing there, unable to move farther without my help, I often reach down, put my arms around the barrel of his chest, pull him toward me, give him a tight hug, kiss him at the soft spot on the left side of his nose, and say, "Mac, you're my best friend" in the same tone Jessica Tandy uses with Morgan Freeman in* Driving Miss Daisy.

*Mac stands there. He doesn't rub against my leg or lift his head to lick my face. Only his eyes move to the back of his head as if to say, "Do you have to do this now?" But I can't help myself. He is so darn huggable.*

*And he is my best friend.*

## Love Letter

I am excited to see Mary. She's been gone a long time. I jump off the sofa and run to greet her. My tail has not stopped wagging to welcome her home when I get an unexpected surprise.

My dear friend Sadie has sent me an AOL message (Aroma On Leasher). I sniff Mary's knee where Sadie shares, "There are lots of leashers at my house. Most of them care more about the drink in their hand than me at their knee." I move my nose to Mary's hind leg. Sadie continues, "You would love it here. Food is sitting on low tables so it's easy to sneak when no one's looking. The nice leashers share their treats with me." Sadie leaves a final message on Mary's ankle. "It would be more fun if you were here. Come see me soon. I miss you." Mary grabs my leash and I'm pulled into the present. I give her a dirty look for not taking me with her to Sadie's house. She avoids my stare.

But I don't stay mad for long. There's a bounce in my step on our last walk of the day as I think about my old friend Sadie.

*I feel like I'm cheating on Mac. I return from a party at Grant's house where I play with his irresistibly sweet golden retriever, Sadie. Like an unfaithful husband with another's lipstick on his collar, I am wracked with guilt. Mac's nose moves over the lower half of my body like a metal detector looking for gold. He pauses at each spot where Sadie's scent lingers. I avoid looking at him, but I sense him giving me a dirty look for being with another dog. I divert his attention with the offer of a walk. Once on the street, the traces of the one who came between us evaporate into the cool evening air.*

## What a Drag

"Mac, I've got something for you," Mary said as she came up the stairs with three Target bags in her hand. My mind started racing: beef jerky, new ball, or that new ice cream some wonderful leasher invented for dogs? Wrong on all accounts. She bought me a new leash. How exciting is that?

It gets worse.

This is not your ordinary leash. Instead of holding it in her hand, Mary wraps it around her waist. So now I have to stay right by her side. If I try to walk ahead, I have to drag her with me, and she's not a small girl. With my old leash it was easy to pull ahead because only the strength of Mary's arm held me back. Now when I pull, she stands still and it's almost impossible to budge her. I get so exhausted that I quit struggling and walk closely by her side.

I have an idea. I start going in circles pretending like I have to poop. Since we're attached at the waist, she goes in circles, too. It's fun watching her spin around like a ballerina on a jewelry box.

But now she's onto me, and she un-clicks the leash from her waist and holds it in her hand like a traditional leash. I hope I've seen the last of that contraption.

*On average, Mac is well trained, but he's a puller. When Mac was a puppy, a man I'd never seen on the street before asked if he could take Mac for a stroll. The stranger took Mac's leash and walked him about three feet, and when Mac pulled, the man turned around and walked him three feet the other way. He completed this imaginary track around a miniature football field several times, forcing Mac to turn around each time he pulled. "This is the way you get him to walk on a leash," he said*

*as he handed leash and puppy back to me. I wish I had taken his advice.*

*To correct this imperfection in grown-up Mac, I tried collars that choke, toggle, and pinch, Gentle Leaders, Easy Leads and harnesses in a variety of styles and materials. Then I read about the "tree" method, where you attach a leash to your belt and if he starts to pull, you plant yourself like a tree and wait for your dog to give you slack in the leash before resuming your walk. The belt thing was a bit nerdy, so I bought a leash made for this purpose.*

*Neither Mac nor I were prepared for our new walking arrangement. The first time I tried the tree method, all was well until Mac decided to charge an azalea bush to smell who had gone before him. Unaccustomed to planting my feet, this "tree" was uprooted and flown through the air by Hurricane Mac, making a crash landing in the chain-link fence behind the bush.*

*The next time his scent indicator took him farther than the length of the leash, I was ready for him. Jerked abruptly and deterred from his mission, Mac gave me an "eat poop" look and tried to charge onward. But I stood firm as the alpha, and he walked back toward me.*

*Mac let me have my way for several blocks before he devised a plan to walk in circles around me until tummy burns forced me to withdraw the noose from around my belly.*

*Then, I added "Tree Method" and $35 to my list of failed attempts to control my pulling pup.*

# A Day in the Life

*"The best thing about tomorrow is*
*it's just another day."*

—Mac

## Morning Routine

I love mornings when my leasher and I first wake up. It's hard to tell who wakes up whom. Sometimes I hear Mary yawn as she stretches her front and hind paws in opposite directions, reaching to touch something that's not there. Other times my wiggles wake her when I wipe the sleep out of my eyes with my front paws. She sits up, scratches me behind my ears, kisses me, and says in a high-pitchy voice, "Good morrrrning. How's my little Boo Bear?" I wag my tail really fast without even trying because I've missed that baby talk voice for the last seven hours. Then comes the best part.

Mary goes to the bathroom to do her "doggy business" and I crawl onto her side of the bed. It's nice and warm and smells like Mary. I curl up into a ball and snuggle with myself. She finishes her business, washes her face, rubs stuff on it, and brushes her teeth while I enjoy the warmth of her spot, knowing she is nearby and not going anywhere for a while. She leaves the bathroom, walks toward the closet, and without fail, says in her baby talk voice, "Are you in my spoooottt?" Again, I wag my tail wildly, which seems to make her happy. She stays in the closet until she finds the right outfit for the day. I think she looks good in everything.

I see her putting on shoes. This is a sign that my time here is almost up. She approaches the bed. With one paw on her hip, she tells me to get off the bed. I stretch and yawn and pretend I don't know what she's saying. She tugs at the covers and acts like she's going to make up the bed with me in it. I give up my position and jump off. I'm sad that my morning routine is over.

But happy that it's time for breakfast.

*"Why don't you meet me in the mornings and we'll do P90X together?"* Laura asks, knowing that my gym membership had expired.

*"No, I can't. Mac and I walk in the morning."*

*"Don't let me interrupt your Mac routine,"* Laura replies, half sarcastic, half joking.

Okay, I admit it. I like my routine, and I don't care if it makes me less spontaneous or interesting.

The word "routine," like so many words in the English language, has both positive and negative connotations. The seesaw of consensus here would likely tilt heavily to the negative end.

People don't want to be routine. It makes you sound less interesting than others who are more free-spirited. Our trusty thesaurus lists *"monotonous, dull, mundane, and humdrum"* among the list of equally boring synonyms. But what if you like, or I dare say, *"love"* your routine?

My *"Mac routine,"* as Laura calls it, is predictably fun. Whether it's knowing he will jump in my spot when I get out of bed each morning, crawl on top of me when I'm doing sit-ups each night, chase a tennis ball anytime and as long as I'm willing to throw it, or magically appear by my desk at 5:00 p.m. to remind me it's time to quit working and feed him, Mac redefines routine.

I wouldn't go as far to say he turns "routine" into its antonym "exciting," like the thesaurus suggests, but the seesaw definition levels out when love jumps on.

## UP

*"Did anyone ever tell you that your dog looks like the dog from* UP?*" asks a stranger at the dog park. "He's so happy!"*

*If you haven't seen* UP, *rent it. The dog in the movie is an animated version of a fairly generic dog, which I suppose could be a Lab. His name is Doug, and he's able to talk because his owner invented a talking collar.*

*Doug is obsessed with squirrels. When he detects one is nearby, he yells, "SQUIRREL!" His eyes enlarge, his tail perks up, his head jerks in the direction of the squirrel, and he freezes. But the most memorable part about Doug is his smile and his ability to make the viewer smile.*

*Though I'd never compared Mac to Doug, the stranger's comparison is a huge compliment. Mac is always happy when he's playing ball. It makes all the other dogs want to run beside him whether they care about the ball or not.*

*Happiness draws you in, whether you're a person or a dog. Happiness breeds happiness, and, unfortunately, sadness attracts sadness. As such, when I'm sad, I grab the leash and a tennis ball and head to the dog park where in minutes Mac is able to turn my down into up.*

## A Day at the Beach

Mary and I are at the beach. I love the beach. I love running as fast as I can to catch a soggy tennis ball before a big white wave takes it away from me. When this happens, I look everywhere for my ball. First I plant my feet and look under my body. I spin to the left... no ball. To the right... no ball. I put my nose to the sand, sniffing with all my might until I find it. That big wave never returns it to the place where he took it from.

I never get hot because waves keep me cool. I'm not crazy about the sand that gets on my tongue and won't leave, but you take the good with the bad.

I remember the first time I went to the beach. I tilted my head back, closed my eyes, and held my nose high to take in the air. It was a smell I had never smelled before. If I wasn't enjoying myself so much, I might have been mad at Mary for not bringing me here before. My nostrils worked overtime, going in and out so fast, trying to keep up with the rapid beating of my heart.

I ran in the sand. Like the air, it was different than the ground at home. It was hot on top and cool underneath. It took on different forms, too. Before I got to the water, the sand didn't stick to my paws. By the water, the same sand was a different color, smell, and texture, and I had to struggle to get it out of the pad cracks of my feet.

But what awed me the most were the waves. They roared and crashed and stood up like a Great Dane on its hind legs and fell on top of whatever was beneath them.

Mary walks close to the water without falling in. She grasps the soaked tennis ball in the cradle of a long, purple, plastic launcher and slings it over my head as far as she can throw. She keeps walking as I run to retrieve my passion. I run back to her, drop the ball at her feet, and sprint ahead to where I think her next toss will land. Launch, retrieve. Launch, retrieve. Launch, retrieve.

We come to a group of rocks that reach into the water like steps to the ocean's basement. We turn around and walk the other way, repeating our rhythm in the other direction until we're back to where we started from.

We walk to the car. Mary rubs my body with an old beach towel, removing the outer layer of sand in my fur before I jump into the back seat of the car. Mary pours me a bowl of water. I can't get enough. She fills the bowl again, and I lap the bottom dry. I get so thirsty at the beach. Mary starts the car and is barely out of park before I'm sleeping like a pup. I don't wake up until we pull into the garage. I'm dog-tired. But it's a good tired, the tired you feel after spending a day just the way you want.

*My favorite place in the world is by the water. I like lakes, but I love the ocean. The water brings me peace whether the world around me is peaceful or not. As the waves crash against the sand and move back into the ocean, I imagine them carrying every worry I have and taking them to a place where I'll never have to experience them again.*

*I love the breeze hitting my face, keeping me cool in the summer and making me shiver in the winter—provided you call 60 degrees winter. I love walking along a coastline arm-in-arm with my thoughts and plans and hopes. Life doesn't get any better than this.*

*But it does.*

*Walking alone versus being with Mac at the ocean is the difference between dreaming about happiness and being happy.*

*If my love of the ocean is a ten on a scale, Mac's is 100. As I look for*

*a place to park along the Pacific Coast Highway, Mac's anticipatory cries
are a cross between fighting cats and growling stomachs. He moves from
side to side in the back seat of the SUV, trying to predict which door will
open first. It takes all my weight to keep him in the car while I attach his
leash. The commands he normally obeys are dust in the wind. All four legs
are airborne as he jumps from the car. He manages a perfect landing before
pulling me forward with oxen strength. I contain my beast long enough to
get my backpack of supplies from the front passenger seat.*

*Our destination is a stretch of beach in Malibu nicknamed "Billionaires'
Beach," a reference to the exclusive homes separating the ocean from the
highway. No two houses are alike. Some are new and multi-story, crafted
of glass and steel, rising from the seashore where $50 million teardowns
once stood. Others with distressed-by-nature clapboard siding stand in the
shadows of their newer neighbors. No matter their size or age, one thing
they all have in common is a fence or garage connecting to neighbors on
either side, forming a mismatched barrier between the highway and the
beach. The only entrance is indicated by a small brown sign reading "Beach
Access." The slight sign signals the existence of a 10-foot white glossy gate
leading to paradise.*

*The only parking is on the shoulder of the immensely busy three-lane
road that connects this wealthy city to the rest of the world. The day of the
week and time of day determine how far we park from the entry. Mac's
determined gait pulls me toward the entrance. His four legs in lockstep, he's
not stopping for anyone or anything. Not even a discarded pizza could keep
him from his mission.*

*We arrive and Mac's feet march rapidly in place while I lean down
to unhook his collar. The second Mac is untethered, he runs with reckless
abandon into the vast Pacific Ocean. His joy becomes my joy, and in that
moment, I am richer than any Billionaire Beach resident.*

## The Psychic

*The last quarter of our two-mile walk around the neighborhood is on Sunset Boulevard, where famous bars, restaurants, a strip club, and ever-changing storefronts line the north and south sides of the street. Today Mac discovers a new proprietor with "Psychic" painted in big purple letters on the glass door. A red neon sign flashes "Open" in the window. He pokes his head into a small room with couches and chairs draped in white-on-white Batik cotton covers. The room is empty. As I pull Mac's leash, a deep sultry voice calls out, "It's okay. I read paws."*

*Madam V appears from behind a stained-glass screen dressed in a purple, gold, and green silk caftan. Her dark hair is wound tightly in a high French twist. Madam V's bright orange lips clash with the turnip-purple polish painted on her fingernails and the toes of her petite bare feet. Her turquoise eye shadow peeks out from behind her dark, thick, fake eyelashes. She looks like a peacock. Mac is in shock, his torso still as his head moves up and down, scanning the body of the woman addressing him.*

*"You read paws." As the words trickle from my lips, Mac sits and rests his right paw on Madam V's outstretched hand. She takes his paw, holds it perpendicular to the floor, and looks intently at the bottom of it. Mac sits motionless, staring at her mountainous hair.*

*"I see reds, oranges, and gold where you lay. I see an aura of love that originates in your heart and permeates the atmosphere encircling the ones you choose to love. I sense the powers you have to dry a tear with your gaze. And I see an In-N-Out bag in the bush outside." Mac darts out the door, pulling me with him, shoves his head in the shrubs, and pulls out the familiar red and white bag of his favorite restaurant.*

## Human Parks

Whether it's Coffee Bean, Peet's, or Starbucks, when two or more leashers enter their park together, they tend to talk to just each other. When alone, they mostly peck on their phones and computers. They usually sit in the same spot but will move if the sun or cigarette smoke gets in their eyes. They drink brown liquids purchased inside glass walls where dogs are not allowed.

I like going to the human parks because I get lots of attention. Leashers also drop a lot of food. Mary and I talk to and sniff other leasher/dog couples.

We met Rollo and Tommy at Coffee Bean & Tea Leaf. I like Rollo. He has a square jaw and is quiet without being boring. He looks like me but he's darker. Mary calls him a *chocolate Lab*, two of her favorite things. I saw Rollo again at the dog park across the street from the human park. Rollo is older and slower than me, which I could tell makes him sad. So I pretended to be slower, too, so Rollo could get to the ball first. Mary figured out what I was doing and threw the ball in Rollo's direction so it wouldn't look so obvious. We're quite the thoughtful couple.

Mary and Tommy have a lot in common aside from their love of Labs (an admirable trait). They're both inventors, which is apparently not a common job for leashers. Tommy invented something for dogs that I'm not allowed to tell you about. Mary's inventions are for humans, so I like Tommy's better. Tommy is a writer like Mary and me. Well, not just like us, since he makes money doing it. Tommy's a neat leasher. If I didn't have Mary, I'd want him to be my leasher because he has a pool. I think Mary likes Tommy, too. She puts extra stuff on her face and lips when we go to Coffee Bean & Tea Leaf.

We met Hank and Sam at Peet's Coffee. Hank is a hound dog, a Redbone Coonhound to be exact. Nothing seems to bother Hank much, except for leashers who push shopping carts or look like the street is their home. If they come close, Hank barks so fast and loud, you'd think there were four of him. If Sam is not there to hold him back, he nearly pulls the metal table he's tied to into the street. Once the unwanted leasher is out of sight, Hank returns to a serene existence.

Hank's leasher Sam is a good picture taker. The first time we met, he took a picture of me, Hank, and another dog and showed it to Mary. Now we time our visits to Peet's when we know they'll be there. It's not hard since they are there every day. Sam writes TV shows and movies. He's going to be famous one day, but I hope not so famous that he doesn't come to Peet's anymore.

But my favorite human park is Starbucks because Jane works there. She is the store's alpha-leasher. When she sees me, she comes from behind the counter and walks outside with a cup of fluffy white cream. She holds it to my mouth, where my eager tongue licks and licks and licks. I continue licking even when I know the cup is empty, because the sides of the shiny white paper cup still smell like some is left. Finally, I concede. Jane gives me a hug and a kiss and I kiss her back while smelling the pocket of her green apron to see if she dropped any cream in it.

*Before I had Mac, I rarely went to restaurants alone because I wasn't comfortable being a party of one. There's something about a person sitting alone with a dog that draws others in. Though not a conscious objective, it became obvious that owning a dog could lead to a party of two.*

*West Hollywood is a dog-friendly city. Thanks to year-round warm weather, almost every restaurant and coffee house has outdoor seating where dog lovers and their four-legged children eat and drink together.*

*In addition to fabulous weather, West Hollywood is also known for its fabulous gay men. With more than forty percent of the population identifying as LGBTQ (Lesbian Gay Bi-Sexual Transgender Questioning) it lessens the dating pool for a SHIFFF (Single Heterosexual Intelligent Full-Figured Female). So when I meet a handsome guy with a dog at Peet's Coffee, I assume he's gay until proven straight.*

*Leave it to Mac to find two smart, handsome, straight, intelligent men in the middle of our gay mecca. One day while waiting for my iced vanilla latte with almond milk, a cute guy tapped me on the shoulder and asked if the yellow Labrador out front was mine. He scared me at first and I immediately looked out the window to make sure Mac was still tied to the parking meter where I left him. Seeing my fright, Sam said, "He's fine. Didn't mean to scare you. I wanted to show you this." On his phone was a picture he had taken of Mac, his own dog Hank, and an unknown mostly black shepherd mix.*

*The photograph captured their profiles taken eye level to the dogs. Mac was farthest from the camera, sitting perfectly still, staring west down Sunset Boulevard. His expression was hard to read. He was either totally Zen or extremely peeved at being tied to a parking meter. Hank, in the middle, was secured to a heavy wire table. He faced the opposite direction, eyes intent on something closing in from the east, daring anyone or anything to walk on his sidewalk. Dog John (or Jane) Doe was closest to the camera, facing west like Mac, ears up, mouth parted, the early detection of a smile. Each dog knew the others were there, but shunned interaction.*

*This was the first of many coffees shared with Sam and Hank. Sam lives close by and is a regular at Peet's between 8:30 and 9:30. There aren't a lot of tables and chairs, so strangers often share a table. But few customers are strangers to Sam. He knows most of the regulars and the not-so-regular customers. If you have time to sit and chat, Sam welcomes you into his conversation with a "Mary, you know Susan, don't you?" It's a warm and friendly gesture, with a true small-town feel.*

*Another favorite dog couple of ours is Tommy and Rollo. We met one Sunday at Coffee Bean & Tea Leaf while I was drinking a latte and reading the paper. Tommy came up to the table, cradled Mac's face in his hands and scratched his neck while Mac showered wet kisses on Tommy's face between his mouth and his nose. The sloppy kind of kisses that, no matter how hard you try, you can't keep your eyes open. Tommy introduced us to his chocolate Lab, Rollo, who was amenable to sharing his master's love. We talked about our love of dogs and their role in our lives as companions and children. As is often the case, I didn't learn his name during our first encounter, only Rollo's.*

*Sometime later, Mac and Rollo met up at a neighborhood dog park, and while launching wood-chip-coated tennis balls to our respective Labs, Tommy and I realized we'd met before. Our conversation expanded beyond our lovable four-legged children.*

*Tommy is a movie and television writer and producer and invited me to a screening of his latest movie. I was so excited. I had my hair blown out and brought my best friend Laura with me. We debated all night long whether the girl beside him was a sister or a girlfriend. We had a lot in common. He was a writer. I'm sort of one. He's an inventor. I am, too. Also, when we met up again to throw balls to our dog boys, we both showed up in vintage cars, mine a 1955 Thunderbird and his a 1973 Ford Galaxie.*

*Tommy moved out of West Hollywood with his fiancé, so it's been a while since we've seen each other. I miss running into him at the dog park, the coffee shop, or Pinkberry. I suppose I could call him, but the premeditation seems invasive. Friendship forged through dogs often revolves around spontaneous encounters.*

*Farther East on Sunset at Starbucks, it's not the patrons that draw me in. It's the friendly people who work there. They have an iced grande soy latte waiting for me when I arrive at the cash register, alongside a short cup of whip, a puppy cappuccino for Mac. The manager of the store fed Mac whipped cream when he was a puppy, and he has never forgotten it.*

*Fortunately, he does not know every Starbucks could do the same.*

## The Happy Companion

*I'm sitting in traffic at the fifth red light in a row when I see a thin man with a leathery face covered in bushy black-and-gray hair pushing a grocery cart on the sidewalk next to me. The man's feet are black from walking barefoot and his dirty, torn, red-and-black checkered flannel shirt is unbuttoned, exposing a soiled, once-white T-shirt. A belt is pulled tight around his skinny waist to keep his baggy pants from falling.*

*His cart is full of over-stuffed plastic grocery bags covering a layer of tin soda cans and plastic water bottles. A torn thin blue tarp is draped over the cart and two bungee cords protect its contents from spilling onto the ground.*

*A light tan, mixed-breed dog tied by a rope to the handle of the grocery cart is keeping pace with his homeless owner. The dog's stance is strong. He holds his head high and swishes his tail from side to side.*

*He's a happy dog.*

*When I've seen homeless people with dogs, I've always felt sorry for the dog. Is he getting enough to eat? Is he safe? Is he treated well? But seeing this proud dog walking beside a grocery cart like he's pulling a golden carriage made me pause.*

*Mac wants three basic things: to eat, be outside, and to always be with me. The dog I'm watching has this all the time. His owner doesn't leave him alone to go to work, the movies, the beauty salon, the gym, or a ballgame. He isn't left in a house all day long with nothing new to smell. And this dog's master probably doesn't jerk his leash when he tries to eat day-old French fries off the street.*

*So who's the happier dog? Mac or the one tied to a grocery cart?*

## Enjoying the Journey

Today, Mary and I took a friend of hers to Manhattan Beach. When I heard "beach," I got REALLY excited! I couldn't wait to chase the ball into the ocean, dive into the waves, dig in the sand, and run without a leash. But I got none of this. Nil, nothing, zero, zilch.

There were two paths; one for leashers and dogs and one for people on wheels. I could see the ocean to my left until we turned around, and then it was on my right. I kept walking at my "gotta get there" pace, but I never got there. I never got my paws wet, never got sand on my tongue, and never felt the wet felt of a tennis ball.

I was annoyed and angry. Why come all this way and not get in the water? But then I started noticing things along the way, and I calmed down. The pretty-smelling rose bushes, the water bowls nice people left outside their doors, the air, surfers, things I don't notice when I'm doing my thing in the ocean. Along the way became *the way*.

After walking a few miles in my new emotional state, we climbed a steep hill to a Coffee Bean & Tea Leaf I'd never been to before. There was a rule that dogs couldn't come on the porch (stupid rule), so Mary tied me to a parking meter. Normally, this would make me mad and nervous to be away from Mary, but more people petted and talked to me when I was on the sidewalk than if I had been on the porch.

My trip to Manhattan Beach made me realize that not getting what you want can make you stumble onto something better.

## Walk On

*Nearing the end of our walk, I press the "Inspiration" playlist on my iPod where* Elvis Presley's Greatest Gospel Hits *is downloaded. "You'll Never Walk Alone" has become my go-to song when I'm feeling down.*

*When you walk through a storm*
*Hold your head up high*
*And don't be afraid of the dark.*
*At the end of the storm*
*Is a golden sky*
*And the sweet silver song of a lark.*

*Walk on through the wind,*
*Walk on through the rain,*
*Tho' your dreams be tossed and blown.*
*Walk on, walk on*
*With hope in your heart*
*And you'll never walk alone,*
*You'll never walk alone.*

*While this Rodgers and Hammerstein show tune was penned for the 1945 musical Carousel, which had nothing whatsoever to do with dogs, the lyrics are eerily relevant for any dog owner.*

*Rain or shine, Mac and I walk. We hear birds chirp in the morning and crickets sing at night. Some days the skies and my spirits are darker than others. But a walk with Mac always brings light to a dark day.*

*And the one thing I never have to do is walk alone.*

## Visitation Rights

*I hear a whimper from behind the ficus-covered, wrought-iron fence that surrounds the lawn of the once empty apartment building. Mac hears it too. He pushes his snout through the four-inch spacing of the metal bars to rub noses with the prisoner behind them.*

*It's a smallish dog. In the dark and overgrown greenery, I see red fur and beautiful but sad brown eyes. I can't make out the sex or the breed, so I call it "her." It makes for a better story.*

*We've never seen this dog during the day. But on our evening walks, she waits in silence for Mac to seek her out. Once she glimpses his strong blond body, she cries out softly enough, ready to retreat in case it's not Mac on the other side.*

*Mac and the jailed lass share a moment. After seconds of nose fondling, Mac continues his journey toward home. Behind the bars, she runs the length of the yard alongside him. He wants to carry on, but is drawn back into her melancholy. He plops his heavy body down and puts his paw through the bars to meet her uplifted limb. They sit holding paws in stillness by the moon's light.*

*It's getting late. I pull Mac's leash to signal an end to this less-than-conjugal visit. We walk home, saddened that we never see her in daylight or beyond the confines of her ficus-fenced cell. I wonder, "Does she get love on the inside?"*

## Night Moves

I try to get comfortable as I move from favorite spot to favorite spot. I begin downstairs where it's cool and I lay in the corner of the sofa that I'm not supposed to. Forbidden furniture is always more comfortable than dog-approved spaces.

After a while, I wander upstairs to see what Mary is doing. I'm in time to watch her perform her evening routine, which makes me glad I'm not a leasher.

Every night, she washes the stuff off her face that she put on that morning and sometimes as recently as that evening. She uses little pads, brushes, and sticks to apply liquid and powder to her face and tar to her eyes, only to take it off before going to bed. It takes a long time to get the stuff off her face, and then she puts on different stuff. I think she's hiding something under all that stuff and checking each night to make sure it's still there before covering it up again.

Next she pulls a thin string out of a plastic box, wraps it around her fingers, shoves her fingers, string and all, into her mouth, and runs the string back and forth between her teeth. Maybe she's digging for food she hid there earlier. On second thought, that's not such a bad idea.

Finally she gets into bed. She opens a book and ignores me. But not for long. She puts the book on the table beside the bed and turns on her side to face me. She scratches my neck and rubs behind my ears. She kisses me in the center of my nose and turns off the light.

The last move of the night.

# Ranting and Raving

*"Give me food, or give me death!"*

—Patrick "Mac" Henry

## Prejudice

Little dogs get all the breaks. As I sit tied to a trashcan, I see a Yorkie go into a Subway cradled in his leasher's arms. As I peer out of the back window of an SUV, I see a Chihuahua carried into the grocery store peeking out of a large fluffy pink purse. I can swear she's sneering at me.

It's not fair. Small dogs get to ride on the plane with their leashers while we big dudes have to travel in a dark dingy cargo area.

Mary is treated unfairly too. Just because I'm 29 inches tall and weigh 85 pounds, she has to pay more at daycare and more at the groomer than a little yappy dog. If you want my opinion, they should be charged more for the irritation factor.

But being a big dog does have its benefits. At least I don't have to wear those stupid-looking tutus and ridiculous holiday sweaters. So there, Chihuahuas, Yorkies, toy poodles, and Pomeranians, take your sequins and Santa sweaters, while I remain, dignity intact, tied to this trashcan.

## Dieting to Fit In

*I was on my patio enjoying the full moon and crisp night with Mac curled up in a circle at the foot of my lounge chair. My evening solitude was abruptly interrupted by the arrival of a blue airport shuttle whose occupants' loud laughter could likely be attributed to the consumption of first-class cocktails.*

*From my reclined position, I caught a glimpse of my neighbor's nephew Herman's bald head above the patio wall. Hearing the rowdiness approach the building, Mac jumped into protective mode, emitting the deafening bark and ferocious growl of an animal trained to attack. Being a frequent visitor, Herman knew the source of the snarl was a lovable Lab attempting to be something he was not. That's when I heard him say through inebriated lips,*

*"Shut up, Fatso."*

*My decision to remain quiet and anonymous immediately changed at this idiot's derogatory reference to Mac's physique. I jumped up from the chaise and forcefully slammed the patio door to let the jerk know I heard his belittling remark. There, I showed him!*

*The next day, I put Mac on a diet.*

We dogs come in all shapes, sizes, and colors. Clyde the English bulldog is almost a square. He weighs 60 pounds and is half my length. Dillon, the collie next door, is larger in size than me but probably doesn't weigh as much. I carry a lot of weight because I'm big-boned. Buster and Charley, Jack Russell terrier brothers, are thin because they are young and run fast. I doubt they slow down to eat. Then there is Homer, the Lhasa Apso/Shih Tzu something or other. No matter how much he eats, he never gains a pound. And he eats all the time. He's so lucky; I hate him.

If I sound obsessed about weight, it's because I am. I didn't used to be but everyone keeps calling me fat. I'm not fat. I'm wearing my winter coat. I see Labs a lot heavier than me. I'm healthy. I get lots of exercise. However, I notice I'm not the first one to get to a tennis ball at the dog park like I used to. Then Mary puts this picture on the refrigerator that shows a yellow Lab with five body types starting with "Underfed" and ending with "Obese." I admit I lean toward the heavier end, but I'm not obese.

And so the fun begins. Mary buys me "lite" food, which has the flavor of cardboard. Next she put away the pigs' ears and now I only get them when I've played ball for a long time. I sure do miss those squiggly, honey-colored, greasy treats. She then starts breaking my treats up into pieces. She thinks I don't know what she's up to. I know I'm not getting the same amount of treats as I used to, even if she's giving me the same number.

I knew it was coming before it happened. Every time we run into a Lab and his leasher, Mary asks, "What food do you feed him? How much do you feed him?"

I get so tired of hearing it all, blah, blah, blah.

Still, it's been a few weeks since she's been starving me and not to brag, but I think I'm thinner. My curves are more pronounced, and my face looks thinner.

I know that eating less is good for me. I'm still not happy about it. But I've got a long life ahead of me, and I don't want to be sick when I'm old. So I'll suck it up for now, well not literally because that would be contrary to my goal.

I'll never possess the sleek body of a Greyhound, or even an American Lab. Stockiness is in my English genes. I'll just be the best that I can be for me.

## Pet Names

My name is Mac Headley Kiser. There's an old dog's tale that leashers have passed down from one generation to the next that dogs' names should be only one syllable so it's easier for us to learn our names. Whether that's true or not doesn't matter, since my leasher has more names for me than Lassie has liver pills.

My personal favorite is Fab Lab. The others are rather annoying. There are variations of my actual name. Mac Attack, Big Mac, Mac & Cheese, Mac Truck, Mac Daddy, and Macalicious.

Then, for some reason, she's decided my alter ego is Boo, which supposedly comes from a Lobo song titled "Me and You and a Dog Named Boo." That creates an entirely new set of names. Boo Boo, Boo Boy, and Boo Bear. There are also slur names regarding my physique, such as Round Mound, Big Boy, and Macadamia Nutless.

When she's in a particular silly mood, I become a lyric: "Hunk-a-Hunk of Burning Mac"; "Boo, Don't Take Your Love to Town"; and "Who's Afraid of the Big Bad Boo?".

It's probably a good thing dogs don't talk with words. Somehow I don't think Mary would find Meal Ticket, Ball Tosser, and Poop Picker Upper that endearing.

## If I Were in Charge

If dogs ruled the world:

- Cats couldn't climb trees and birds would be more approachable so we could get to know each other better.

- Refrigerators wouldn't have doors.

- Bushes wouldn't die because you peed on them.

- Tennis balls would never get lost.

- Bones would never run out of meat.

- Leashes would be made of beef jerky.

- Cars would be made of sponge.

- The temperature would always be 75 degrees.

- Car windows wouldn't roll up.

- Big dogs could go to Nordstrom, too.

- Animals would be required to sit on the sofa.

- Groomers wouldn't exist.

- Poop would be a perfume.

- Eating and sleeping would be a sign of intelligence.

- Leashers would never have to work so they could play with us all day.

That's the way it would be if I were in charge.

## Liar

Mary is lying to me. She keeps telling me she doesn't have a ball. Viking knows she's lying, too. He smells it. I smell it. I want to get the ball before he does. She's my leasher, dog gone it, so I deserve the ball.

I bark louder. Mary and Sandra, Viking's leasher, can't understand why we can't keep our noses out of Mary's pants pockets. I bark louder.

"Mac, I don't have a ball! What's wrong with you?" Mary replies, almost angrily.

What do you mean what's wrong with me? You're the one who has a tennis ball and won't give it to me. And then you lie to my face. I'm the one who should be angry.

*I got home around 10:00 p.m. and grabbed the leash and keys to take Mac out for his last walk for the night. At the end of the sidewalk, we ran into Sandra and Viking, out for their good-night poops as well. Instead of rummaging through the bushes for food, playing run-around-the-butt with Viking, or scent sampling every shrub, Mac stands by my side, tilts his head up to look me in the eyes, and barks.*

*"What's wrong with you?" I ask. He continues with desperation in his bark. Mac and I have been together long enough that I know what he wants by the tone of his voice, and this pitch had, "Give me the ball!" written all over it.*

*"Mac, I don't have a ball. What's wrong with you?" I reply irritably. Then Viking begins to howl as they both keep poking the side of my leg with their noses. That's when it hit me. I'd just come from playing tennis, and the fragrance of tennis balls lined my pockets.*

*If only my $50-per-ounce perfume worked as well on men as ninety-nine cent tennis balls do on dogs.*

## I Want Food

Dog gone it, Mary! You keep feeding me less. You throw away things that I would love to eat. This has got to stop. You stand at the counter and eat part of the chicken from the bone and then what do you do? You throw the bone away. I would *kill* to chew the meat off the bone and eat the insides. It smells so good, and I'm so hungry. I tried to grab it out of the trash without you seeing me, but that eye in the side of your head caught me. You are starving your only dog to death.

It's bad enough you won't feed me, but you won't even let me eat food I find on my own. This morning on the way to school, I struck gold in the purple flowered bush behind Pinches Tacos. I smelled a bone. Not as fresh and meaty as the one you threw away last night, but still an honest-to-goodness, bona fide chicken bone. I went in for the kill. You pulled my leash, but you were too late. I had it locked in my jaws. Then *you* got mad at *me* and pulled *my* bone out of my teeth. What is it with you? What is wrong with you? Don't you want me to be happy and full? I guess not.

Well, I love chicken bones, and there is nothing you can do about it. I will continue to sniff, hunt, and dive for any hen remnant around. You can try, but my nose is quicker than your eye. My teeth are stronger than your fingers. You leave me no choice. This is Chicken Bone War, Mary, and I have an army of senses on my side. You have only a leash.

*Mac loves to eat, and is especially fond of chicken. If I don't shut the door and push the button fast enough, he has his head in the trash compactor attempting to pull out chicken bones. Laura once stopped by with a whole roasted chicken from the market. She went upstairs for a few minutes and*

117

*when she came downstairs, the entire chicken was gone, carcass and all. There wasn't a trace of the bird, just the cleanly licked black plastic tray that held what was supposed to be her dinner.*

*I am typically a sucker for Mac's sad, hungry eyes, but eating chicken bones is non-negotiable. While some bones are good for dogs' teeth, chicken bones crack and splinter and can cause internal injuries. I watched Mac carefully after his counter-surfing chicken buffet, but he was unaffected by his poultry conquest.*

*People ask me if I leave food out for Mac during the day. "Are you kidding?" I can't remember him ever leaving food in his bowl. I think he would eat a thirty-pound bag of dog food in one sitting if I let him.*

*If I'm not paying attention, Mac turns our morning walks into bush-diving smorgasbords. I can't help but laugh, seeing his wiggling butt sticking out of a shrub. He emerges from the vegetation with dirt all over his head, a smile on his face, and, if successful, food in his mouth. I let him savor his victory if he finds something soft like pizza or tacos, but if he finds a bone, I pry it from his clenched teeth. It doesn't make him very happy, and he emits a rumbling grunt, his version of \*#@! you, but sometimes making your dog happy has to take a back seat to keeping him healthy.*

## Lamp Shades and Lost Balls

Last night Mary and I spent the night at Sammy Jo's house with her leashers Ron and Jack. Sammy Jo and I rested on the floor while the leashers watched movies.

We had lots of treats thanks to leftovers and gifts from Sammy Jo's birthday party. Her leashers are already planning next year's party, calling it her *quinceañera*. They want a cat piñata.

This morning Sammy Jo and I took the leashers for a walk. I enjoyed it because there were lots of great smells from last night's rain. Sammy Jo walks real slow so I got to take my time. It's different from my street. There are no sidewalks, just roads. We had to be extra careful when cars came. There isn't much grass, so I smelled a lot of tar and tires. It's a nice change for me. I wouldn't want it every day, but I like the variety.

Toward the end of our walk, we saw a dog with a lamp shade on its head like the one Mary tried to make me wear when I broke my leg or when she had my balls cut off (I still haven't forgiven her for that).

As we got closer, we saw why she was wearing the lamp shade. Her face was a mess. All her fur was gone. There were crusty scabs all over her head. She didn't seem to be in pain now, but it must have hurt bad when it happened.

"Do you think she was burned?" Mary asked.

"It looks that way, or maybe a face lift," responded Ron.

"Or a chemical peel gone bad," Mary replied jokingly.

Mean talk. Sammy Jo and I shared disgusted looks. For all we know, the poor gal could have gotten this way rescuing someone from a burning building.

Only leashers do stupid things to their faces for vanity. They get doctors to stick needles in their foreheads and knives in their tummies.

It's all over the E! Channel. I'm proud to say dogs have more sense than that. Vanity pretty much goes out the window when I stop in the middle of the street and lick my balls, or should I say, lick the empty sack where my balls should be.

# The Sad Side of Puppy Love

*"This is a good day to die."*

—Low Dog, Oglala Sioux chief

## Sammy Jo

I laughed when Sammy Jo started wearing Disney Princess diapers. They're made for two-legged babies, but Ron and Jack rigged them to fit Sammy Jo because she drips from her hiney. The diapers aren't funny anymore.

I get sad watching Sammy Jo try to get up or walk or go to the bathroom. One of her leashers carries her outside, holds her under her front paws with her back to his stomach, and squeezes her belly to make her pee. Everyone laughed the first time they saw this. It's not funny anymore. When no leashers are around, I talk to Sammy Jo about her "situation."

"Why do you let them do this to you? Why don't you call it a life and move on?"

In her gentle way, she tells me, "They need me. I do it for them. They're not ready to let go. It's not so bad. You'll understand one day. The older you get, the more you love your leashers, and you do things you would never do as a pup."

"How long will you let this go on?"

"I don't know. One day I'll see it in their eyes, and I'll know it's time. Until then, let's all have a good laugh at my expense. I don't mind."

🐾 🐾 🐾 🐾

*Ron and Jack asked me to keep Sammy Jo while they went to Vegas for the weekend. I thought I was up for the task. I was wrong.*

*They left for the airport around 10:00 a.m. and I let myself into their house to pick up Sammy Jo early in the afternoon. She was lying on a cushioned geriatric dog bed by the fireplace when I arrived. I opened the door, called her name, and saw her balding tail wag briskly back and forth at the sound of my voice. She tried to get up, but couldn't. The claws on her front paws clicked the hearth as she fought unsuccessfully to pull herself up. The effort to stand exhausted her. She leaned her head against the fireplace and her body shifted on its side.*

*I knelt beside her, encircled her upper torso with my arms, and pulled her weak but heavy frame upright. With my arms still hugging her body, I buried my nose into the side of her soft neck and rested there a moment. Her mouth was agape to assist her labored breathing.*

*I switched my grip to around her belly and lifted her to a standing position. The look on her face was fatigued, yet grateful. She stood there a moment enjoying the bliss of being vertical. She tried to walk, but her feeble limbs caved as if there were no bones in her legs.*

*After nearly an hour, lots of sweat and more than a few tears, I got her into the back of my SUV. I called ahead and asked my friend Buddy to meet me at the house to help me get Sammy Jo out of the car.*

*Buddy lifted the back of the SUV and saw the weary diapered dog lying on her side, unable to move. "Why are they doing this?" Buddy asked. I chose to make it a rhetorical question.*

*We carried Sammy Jo on her blanket-covered cushion, Cleopatra style, into the house. Once inside, she was easy to care for until it was time to take her out. I'd seen Ron and Jack help her empty her bowels by holding her up and squeezing her bladder. But I can hardly locate my own bladder, much less a dog's, and I'm not as strong as them. I called a neighbor to come help me carry Sammy Jo's frail but still sixty-pound body outside a couple times a day.*

*After the second day of this unnatural routine, Buddy voiced what I'd been thinking. "Mary, this is serious. You need to call Jack and Ron." Reluctantly, I called them, described Sammy Jo's deteriorating health, and asked them to catch an earlier flight home.*

*It was an anxious flight back to L.A. and they got to my house as soon as they could. After a tearful reunion, they carried Sammy Jo outside and commenced with the bathroom and diaper process. Shockingly, though, they said Sammy Jo was no different than when they left her on Friday.*

*But for Ron and Jack, something was different. The hard façade of their denial had been cracked. They were forced to face reality. They were losing Sammy Jo.*

The last time I saw Sammy Jo, she was lying on her side on a bed beside the fireplace. There were bandages on her front paws because she'd rubbed them bloody from scooting in circles trying to get comfortable. She was still wearing Disney Princess diapers because she couldn't control when she peed and pooped. There was a big oozy bump on her back that looked painful, but was the least of her problems.

I walked over to her, and she didn't move. After a few moments, she could tell I was there and raised her head for a few seconds before it plopped back down. Her goofy smile and the twinkle in her eyes were gone, and in a week she would be too.

Mary is sad. I hear her talking to Ron and Jack on the phone, asking if they're okay. She hangs up and starts crying. I lie on my back and stretch. She smiles and scratches my belly. I succeed in distracting her from sadness. I'm sad, too. But I'm also happy that Sammy Jo isn't a sick dog in Disney Princess diapers anymore.

We go over to Sammy Jo's house. Her bed is not on the floor. Her high feeding bowls are not in the kitchen. I smell around. Her scent is here, but she isn't. Jack is telling Mary about their trip to the vet. Ron is lying on the couch holding Sammy Jo's collar. I think he's crying.

My powers are not strong enough to distract his pain.

## Remembering Patrick

*"When you get settled, I need to tell you something,"* Laura said in an uncharacteristically serious tone.

I had just returned to Los Angeles after a week in Virginia with my family. Laura stayed at the house with Mac while I was gone. We talked every few days while I was away, and nothing in her phone voice had indicated anything was wrong.

*"Okay,"* I responded inquisitively, wondering what could be the source of this seemingly grave conversation. I dragged my heavy suitcase upstairs to my bedroom, took a quick shower, and changed into comfy sweats, both a welcome relief after sixteen hours of driving, waiting in airports, and flying.

When I got downstairs, the aroma of Laura's spicy arrabiata sauce filled the room. Mac was on the floor with both front paws cradling a stuffed bone, licking desperately to get every bit of the artificial bacon and cheese stuffing. I kissed him on the head but got no reaction. Anything edible typically outranks me. Laura handed me a glass of wine as I cozied into the corner of the sofa.

*"Cooper's dad Patrick is dead."*

It felt like my heart stopped. I opened my mouth but nothing came out.

*"He was crossing Crescent Heights. A car ran a red light and hit him. He was killed instantly."*

Reading one of the many thoughts running through my mind, she said, *"Cooper wasn't with him."*

*"When did this happen?"* was all I managed to ask.

*"I'm not sure. It was daylight. He'd been at Sushi Dan for lunch with a friend. They were walking back this way. They had the 'Walk' sign, but a car tried to make the light, hit another car, and he was trapped underneath. You know how bad that intersection is. The other guy was injured, but he's going to make it."*

126

*I took a sip of wine and sat alone with my thoughts. Cooper, a copper-color Vizsla, was a few months younger than Mac, and both had early morning schedules. Patrick and Cooper were the first person and dog we saw every morning. We exchanged pleasantries but few details.*

*I thought Patrick was cute in a messy teddy bear sort of way. He was always smiling and sometimes hung over. His button-up shirt was usually one button off, and his full head of hair rarely combed.*

*Now I was never going to see him again.*

*Tears streamed down my face. Mac looked up from his bone and saw me crying. He went back to licking his bone, but his caring side got the best of him. He jumped up on the sofa and curled up beside me, resisting the urge to pull away when my arms tightly encircled his neck. "Who has Cooper?" I asked.*

*"He's with a neighbor temporarily until they find a permanent home for him."*

*As weeks passed, I couldn't stop thinking about Patrick. This was obviously a sad situation, and I reflected on the reasons I was so affected. This was a guy whose last name I never knew, but I felt a connection to him because of the way he treated his dog and the way he treated me. He had such a positive, lovable spirit, and I missed him.*

*About a month after his death, his friends had a memorial service for Patrick at Hamburger Mary's, one of his favorite hangouts in West Hollywood. His sweet Irish Catholic mom and two of his many siblings flew in from Boston. Family and friends shared fun and poignant stories about Patrick. It made me happy to learn that this man I barely knew was the person I thought he was.*

## Brandon

Brandon was a thirteen-year-old Sheltie whose leasher Kathy works at my daycare. Kathy has pretty white fur on her head and gives me soft treats when no one is looking.

I knew something was wrong when we left Hollywood Hounds Thursday evening. Brandon's body was shaking back and forth and up and down. Kathy was crying, and Frank, the man who loves to play ball with me, tried to comfort them both. Frank told Mary that Brandon was having seizures.

I barked at Mary to throw the ball like I always do when she comes to pick me up. I didn't want to face the fact that I was losing a friend. I hoped that by acting normal, things would be normal, and Brandon would be okay. Mary thought I was being rude and selfish. I can see how she would think that, but I don't like to see friends die. I had just lost my friend Sammy Jo.

I'm going to miss Brandon. I remember the first time we met. It was my first day at Hollywood Hounds. A Great Dane was slobbering all over the floor and a Pomeranian was yapping as I clung to Mary, not wanting her to leave me. Brandon strolled over to me and smelled my butt, though the short legs of his little body would hardly allow his nose to reach. As we traded positions for me to return the favor, he paused, looked at me with his tiny little eyes and silently told me I would be okay, and I was.

*I stopped by Hollywood Hounds today to check on Brandon, and as I suspected, he died last night. Dogs live a tenth of the life we do, but recently I've lost as many friends as dogs. Sammy Jo and Brandon were old, lived good lives, and brought great joy to their owners.*

*Like Patrick, my human friends Marque and Jimmy died too young. Marque was only 39. He had a lot more living to do until cancer said differently. Jimmy killed himself. How did he get to that point?*

*Dogs don't do that. No matter how bad they're treated, they don't throw themselves in front of a car or jump off a bridge. They continue thinking that the next person who comes their way will pet them, feed them, and love them.*

*How can we give people similar hope?*

## A Message from Nike

We all knew it was coming. She lived a good life and longer than anyone thought she would. When Nike's back legs gave out, her leasher, Rose, had a cart made for her. When Nike's front legs gave out, Rose bought her a wagon.

Yesterday Rose had a memorial service for Nike. There was lot of good food. I like memorial services. I ate too much.

Rose put all of Nike's dog friends' names on balloons that floated up to heaven. Rose wanted Nike's friends to welcome her when she got there.

I tossed and turned in my sleep last night. Partly because I ate too much. But partly because I wanted to know where heaven was? I woke Mary up and made her take me outside to do my doggy business.

When we got back in bed, my tummy felt so much better. I fell fast asleep and had a dream. In my dream, Nike told me about heaven.

"Mac, I can't wait for you to get here. It's so much fun. Everything up here makes sense, but it's hard to put into barks you'll understand down there. I want you here, but it's okay that you're there. It's all alright. Life is bright. Everything glows. Tennis balls, Frisbees, dogs, leashers, and bones shine like the reflection of sun on a lake. The grass stays green even when I pee on it. I don't even mind the sprinklers. The sky is blue and it's always sunny. And you know those once-a-year rainbows that leashers get so excited about? We have them every day. The alpha leasher here has a beard and wears a long sheet. He looks like that leasher you bark at on Sunset."

"'Welcome Nike. I have something for you,' he said when I arrived. 'I've been expecting you.' He ducked behind a cloud and grabbed a bundle of balloons. The first one I saw was a blue one with your name on it. Thanks for that.

"OMG, the best part is I have four strong legs! I take running and jumping for granted, which is why I almost forgot to tell you. No more carts or wagons for me.

"I see my Mom crying. It doesn't make me sad like you would think. As sad as she is now, that's how happy she'll be when we're together again, hand to paw. That's the way it works. On those days when Mom thinks she can't take it anymore, I smile my big beautiful smile because I know she can. Yes, it's all alright."

## Nine Days

**Day 1 – Sunday**
Mac: My ear is itching.
Mary:  Yuck, your ear looks nasty. I'll take you to the vet tomorrow.

**Day 2 – Monday**
Dr. H: Give us 30 minutes. We'll get that ear cleaned up.
Mary: Please check out the bump on Mac's hip.
Vet Tech: The doctor wants to talk to you.
Mary: Did he say Cancer? Serious? Surgery?
Mac:  Why is Mary crying? Why is she hitting the bed with her fists? Why does she keep hugging me so tight?

**Day 3 – Tuesday**
Mary: Mac, I love you. You can't leave me.
Mac: Something's not right. I'm tired.

**Day 4 – Wednesday**
Mary: Do you agree with this prognosis?
Oncologist: I'll need to see the lab reports.
Mac: I still don't get all the tears.

**Day 5 – Thursday**
Mary: I'm numb.
Mac: I'm scared.

**Day 6 – Friday**
Front Desk: We'll call you when he's out of surgery. Please sign here.
Dr. H: I found another lump. The biopsy is positive. I'm going to remove it too.
Mary: When will I know something?
Mac: I feel woozy.

**Day 7 – Saturday**
Mary: (on the phone and to neighbors) We should have the results back Monday or Tuesday.

**Day 8 – Sunday**
Mac: Give me more pills.
Mary: I love you Mac.

**Day 9 – Monday**
Doctor H: I think we got it all. His organs are clean.
Mary: Thank God. Mac, I love you so much.
Mac: Is it time for another pill?

## Black Monday

*I still feel the fear from hearing the word. Cancer. I took Mac to the vet for an ear infection and left with a stake in my heart. I tried not to cry when I heard the diagnosis because Mac is so sensitive, and I didn't want him to know how sad I was. I hugged Mac tight for a long time. I never wanted to let go of him.*

*I tried to silence the thoughts in my head and control the panic in my gut to concentrate on what Dr. H was saying as he explained the three levels of mast cell tumors. Like human cancer, there are stages to describe the severity. Level One is the least serious with Three being the worst. Dr. H reluctantly prepared me for the worst since the tumor had appeared so quickly. I burst into tears. The doctor, who I had never seen before, hugged me and didn't pull away even after my mascara discolored his chambray blue scrubs.*

*I drove home numb. I came home to a mess. I was in shock.*

*It was a Monday, and I had just returned home from a weekend in San Diego where I purchased space at an event to sell FoldFlops, portable, folding sandals for women and men, the first of my inventions to market. The event was an underwhelming success and the boxes of FoldFlops I intended to sell in San Diego were stacked four-high in my living room and dining room, creating a boxed maze to reach the sofa.*

*Harley, the smallish white Lab Ron and Jack had recently rescued, was staying with Mac and me for the day while Ron was out of town and Jack was working. I was tired from the weekend and didn't feel like having a houseguest, but Ron and Jack had kept Mac while I was out of town, so I could hardly say no.*

*Harley, while a sweet dog, is needy, and she's a barker. When Mac and I returned home from the vet, Harley demanded attention that I was incapable of giving. I needed to be comforted, not the comforter. At every unfamiliar sound, she barked incessantly. I needed for her to shut up.*

*I called Jack. With tears streaming down my face, my voice cracking and my hand shaking as I held the phone, I told him the news.*

*"I'll be right there. What can I bring you for lunch?" It was a rare occasion that I turned down something to eat, but I wasn't hungry.*

*"Nothing, I'm fine." But I wasn't fine, not fine at all.*

*Harley barked when the doorbell rang and continued her shrill yapping as Jack walked in through the labyrinth of cardboard boxes. I tried to say "hello," but the words wouldn't come. I fell into his strong arms and cried like a baby.*

*I felt better. Crying helped, as did time in Jack's embrace. When I felt strong enough to let go, I realized for the second time that day, my mascara had temporarily ruined a man's shirt. It's a testament to Lancôme Cosmetics that there was anything left on my lashes.*

*Jack stayed as long as work would permit. With him gone, I had no one to distract me from my sadness. Exhausted from the weekend and the morning, I decided to take a nap, yearning to have Mac cuddle up next to me. Harley was having none of it. She barked until I let her join us on the bed, which made Mac jump off and retreat to the stuffed chair in the corner of my bedroom.*

*Days were getting shorter, so when I woke from my fitful nap it was almost dark. I took Mac and Harley for a walk where she barked at all the dogs and people I like to stop and talk to. It was probably just as well, since I didn't feel like talking.*

*Back in the house, I tried to feed Mac, but Harley charged his bowl so I put her in the powder room with her dinner and shut the door. I intended to leave her there so I could have some alone time with Mac, but after she cleaned her bowl, the barking began again.*

*I called Jack to see when he was coming home. Regrettably, he said he would be a while. "How is everything? Are you feeling better?"*

*"Fine," I lied as I pressed the end call button on my phone and threw*

*it across the room. I sat in the corner of the sofa and cried as I looked at the walls of boxes surrounding me.*

*I decided to regain my living space by taking the cartons of FoldFlops to a storage area in the garage. Perhaps clearing the mess in the house would clear my head.*

*Upon returning from each run to the storage unit, I heard Harley barking inside the house. Halfway through the boxes, I gave up my quest to clear the house and plopped down on the sofa. I patted the cushion for Mac to jump up beside me. Instead I got Harley who growled at Mac as he tried to take his rightful place on the sofa.*

*That was it. I'd had it. I ran up the stairs, threw myself down on the bed and wailed, beating the mattress with my fists. I screamed and cussed and cried some more. I picked up the phone and called Jack. He answered, but I couldn't speak. I was hyperventilating.*

*"You have to come home now!"*

*"What's happened?"*

*"You have to come home. Please come home. Please come home," I repeated, sobbing in desperation.*

*Jack got to the house in minutes to find me somewhat composed. I had trouble expressing what I was going through because I didn't know myself.*

*All I knew was that I wanted to be with my dog, and my dog alone.*

*Jack and Harley left, and I hugged Mac tight for a long time. I never wanted to let go of him.*

*Time has passed and Mac is cancer free. But Jack and I often talk about that day when the perfect storm blew over my house; the news of Mac's cancer, a cluttered house, a disappointing weekend, and a dog that wouldn't stop barking. Whatever troubles come my way, Jack reminds me that it's never as bad as what has affectionately become known as "Black Monday."*

## Boots

I'd never seen him cry before. And I'd never seen him without Boots. Boots' leasher, Asa, fought back tears as he spoke softly to Mary.

"We were walking early this morning, around 5:00. It was starting to get light when I saw a blur out of the corner of my eye coming from around a parked truck on the street. There were two large dogs, and the girl walking them couldn't control them. I tried to pick Boots up, but one of the dogs grabbed him in its mouth and shook him from side to side like a little rag doll. I tried to pry its mouth open, but I couldn't get Boots out of its clenched teeth. I screamed for the girl to do something. She had long blonde hair. I've never seen her before. She cried, 'I don't know what to do. They're not mine. I'm just watching them.' The dog finally dropped Boots. I scooped him up and took him to the hospital. I asked the girl to leave her information at my door, but I haven't heard anything."

I don't see how this can end well. Boots is small even for a Yorkie. His bark is loud because it has to be. Otherwise, you don't know he's there. Leashers and dogs on Havenhurst know and love Boots, but these dogs Asa is talking about are strangers. They don't know that Boots' bark is just an act.

I pretended to find something to eat in the grass to avoid seeing the pain and tears in my leasher's eyes. As I glanced up, I saw Mary's and Asa's chins hugging their chests and tears rolling down their cheeks. For the first time, the man with the tennis-ball-colored hair looked old.

Softly, Mary asked, "What do the doctors say?"

"There's been internal bleeding. They don't think he's going to make it. They're keeping him heavily sedated because they don't want him to move, and he would be in a lot of pain."

As the week wore on, I had to continue to fake interest in more grass. Each report sounded more hopeless than the one before it. Asa and his friend Betsy visited Boots every day but weren't allowed to stay long. Boots would get excited when he saw them, which would only cause him to be in more pain. It's hard when all you want to do is see someone, but it's the worst thing you can do for them.

A week from the day of the attack the vet told Asa, "I think it's time."

When the time came, Asa said, "No, don't do it."

"But I've filled out the paperwork," the doctor said.

In his feeble voice Asa said, "I told him 'no'."

When Boots came home, he couldn't feel anything from the middle of his belly to the end of his body. He couldn't walk or tell Asa when he had to do doggy business because he didn't know himself. They rarely came outside and when they did, Asa carried Boots on a towel. Asa would sit down and let Boots' friends say hello, but Boots had empty eyes.

"He should be put down," some of the leashers would say. I'm not exactly sure what that means, but when they said it, they'd get sad looks in their eyes.

Then things started getting better. Boots now comes outside more often, like he did before the attack. His back legs won't move, but his front legs are strong. They pull the rest of his body down the sidewalk. He sure can move fast for a dog with only two good legs. Boots also goes to therapy every week. Not the therapy that Mary goes to where she sits and talks about her life, which puts me to sleep. Boots' therapy is swimming in a pool.

Today Boots came out with his body hitched to a wagon. It's actually a cart that Asa straps him into so that his back legs become wheels. He doesn't go any faster than he does with two legs, but the cart keeps his hind legs from dragging on the sidewalk. Asa says the cart keeps his legs where they're supposed to be. Asa hopes by putting Boots' legs in the cart, they will start to work on their own.

Boot's legs are not the same as before the attack, but his spirit is, whether we like it or not. He's hissing at Mary like he used to and challenging Caviar to a barking war when they see each other. In fact, he may be even meaner than he was before, not that I can blame him.

All of this is pretty amazing for a four-pound Yorkie who wasn't given much of a chance to live. Whenever I get angry because Mary won't throw the ball anymore, I think of Boots and all the pain he's gone through, and I feel grateful that I get to chase a ball with all four legs.

# The World Revolves
# Around Me

*"It's my food, my ball, my Mary."*

—Mac, whenever another dog comes to visit

## Reunited

*I'm trying not to cry as I pass mothers pushing jogging strollers, biking triathletes pumping their pedals to make it up the hill, and morning hikers exercising with their iPods or chatting in pairs.*

*"Mac," I holler for what seems like the hundredth time as I walk alone up and down the steep slope at the top of Runyon Canyon. "Have you seen a yellow Lab?" I ask everyone I pass.*

*"Are you looking for a white dog?" yells a girl with blonde hair from the other side of the canyon.*

*My heart starts beating again, "Yes."*

*"He's down there." I look deep into the dirty brush-covered canyon in the direction she's pointing but can't see a thing. I run down the hill to where she is but don't see him.*

*"He was there a minute ago." We cup our hands over our eyes to block the heat and glare of the sun. Other hikers stop to assist in the search.*

*"There," yells a buff guy in a tank top holding a toy poodle.*

*I see Mac's chubby body trying to climb up the hill in the direction that I'd just come from. I start to run back when the blonde girl says, "He's going back down. I think you're going to have to go down and get him."*

*I look down into the canyon. There are two ways to reach Mac. One is to run to the bottom and walk through the brush to where we see him now. But I'll lose sight of him. I can tell he is disoriented and I don't want to risk losing him again. The other option is to go straight down from where I'm standing. I can keep an eye on him, and it will be quicker.*

*I choose the shortest route down a pathless hill of dried, overgrown brush. I take baby steps, but the soil is loose and I fall several times. My hands are covered in stickers from brushing the heavy thicket out of the way. I surrender trying to walk. I plop down on my butt and bounce down the hill, as a dust-laden whirlwind surrounds me. I feel dirt and pebbles invading my shoes, underwear, and bra. I call out to Mac as I continue my bumpy slide down the hill.*

*Nature's incline levels off and the dust settles. I see Mac. Filled with relief and covered in dirt, I yell for him. My voice cracks and the tears I've held back for the last hour roll freely down my cheeks.*

*I crouch to greet my boy bounding toward me. He licks me on the mouth and face with such force that I fall on my butt once again. He stops and stares at me. In that still look I read, "I'm sorry. I'll never do it again. I love you. Let's go home."*

Where is she? I hear her calling my name but when I go toward her, I hear her yelling from the other direction. I'm hot. I'm thirsty. I've got blue and yellow flowers sticking to me. I think there's one in my eye, but I can't get it out. "Mac," I hear in the distance. I can tell that Mary is getting worried, and I hear her asking, "Have you seen a yellow Lab?" Seconds later, "Have you seen a yellow Lab?"

If only I could tell her where I am, but I'm not exactly sure. I came down the hill to get my tennis ball, and like the ball, time slipped away from me. It was easy following the ball down the canyon, but it's a lot of work trying to get back up. I didn't realize how far down the canyon I was.

I am so hot. Why did we come at this time of the day? I don't like this heat. I like being outside but not when it's this hot. Where is my ball? Where is Mary? I'll go this way. No, maybe she's *that* way. I don't know where I am. It's too hard to climb back up the hill in this heat, and I don't know where down leads. So I keep going up.

"Mac!" Wait a minute. Mary's voice sounds close, close enough to touch. I look toward her voice. She's sliding down the opposite side of the canyon on her butt. She's coming fast, almost as fast as my tennis ball, but she's not rolling over and over, at least not yet. She's telling me to walk down. Oh good. This is easy. I can do it. She's still sliding and dust is clouding the air above where she's sliding. I run down the hill. She's still sliding. Rocks are rolling along beside her.

I hope she's not mad. She doesn't sound mad. She actually sounds happy. She sounds happy, but she's crying. We meet. She's hugging my neck and kissing me.

I hear clapping. Mary and I look up to the high ridge where many people are clapping for us. I give her a kiss on the lips and nose in one tongue sweep. She puts me on my leash, and we walk out of the canyon together.

I still don't have my ball. But for once, I don't care.

## Late-Night Party

Last night we had a fun party at our house. We'd taken our last walk for the evening. It was a full moon and Mary wanted to stay outside, so I let her throw the ball to me on the walkway by our house. We heard voices on the other side of the gate. Mary went to see who was there, and that's when the fun began.

A cute man (according to Mary) in a big yellow coat, with matching hat and pants, ran toward us. "Did you call 911 to report a fire?" he asked. Behind him, big red trucks with colorful spinning lights lit up the neighborhood and blocked the street. Shocked and hardly knowing what to say, a rarity for her, Mary replied, "No."

"Are you Number 9?"

"No, I'm Number 10."

Hey, what do you mean, "*I'm*?" What am I, chopped liver? I live here too. The man in the yellow rubber outfit ran next door. Mary was propping open the gate when a man in matching blue pants and shirt with a patch on his sleeve approached Mary. He had shiny black boots and lots of stuff hanging on his belt.

"Can I come in?" he said.

Um, man with strong arms; I decided to take advantage of this situation. I ran to get a ball. Before letting him into *my* house, I dropped the tennis ball at his feet. He picked it up and threw it down the sidewalk. I retrieved it in time to get back to the door to find more guys in yellow outfits and blue suits coming up the walk.

Mary called the ones dressed in yellow *firemen* and the ones dressed in blue *policemen*. I call them all *ball throwers*.

I dropped the ball and one of the firemen threw it. I had him where I wanted him. Stay out here. There's no fire in there, I promise. Stay out here and play with me. The others have everything under control.

But they charged into the house and upstairs to Mary's closet that has a ladder to the roof. Her closet was not big enough to hold Mary, two firemen, and three policemen, so one stayed behind to pitch the ball to me. I didn't complain.

The excitement lasted about forty-five minutes before the yellow team stripped off their top coats, hopped back onto their trucks and away they went. I hauled my tired body up to bed and fell asleep with visions of uniformed men dancing in my head.

I think Mary did too.

## Sloppy Thief

His eyes look like the ones I bite off the stuffed animals Mary buys me. In the middle of his face is a smudge where a nose should be. When he drinks out of my bowl, there's water all over the floor. And he makes funny sounds all the time.

Now look at him. He's on *my* chair with *my* leasher. His leasher is sitting right there. Why doesn't he sit on her lap? Uh oh, where's he going now? He's in my toy box. No, no you can't have that.

I grab my stuffed hedgehog from him and growl. Yeah, I can growl. Sure, I'm an easygoing Lab, but when some bulldog comes into my house and tries to take over my things, I'm going to stand up for myself. Mary told me that she had a surprise for me, and then this bulldog shows up. Whatever happened to traditional surprises, like bones and balls and squeaking giraffes?

This "surprise" has a name. It's Clyde. I like Clyde when I see him on the street. We often share a bush or two. But you don't realize what a dog is like until you let them into your home. Mary and Clyde's leasher settle in and start watching a movie, but I can't relax. I don't know when he is going to slobber all over my favorite toy.

The movie ends. Mary and I walk Clyde and his leasher to their car. I can relax now. My toys and bones are safe.

Some things are better admired at a distance. Clyde is one of them.

## Playtime

Mary likes to get down on the floor and play with me. She lays out a long narrow blue mat. Then she lays on her back so I can lick her face. She puts her paws behind her head, looks into her belly and crunches up.

That's when I spring into action and jump on her tummy. She tries to keep coming up but I prevent her with my body. It's a game we like to play. She laughs and laughs and then does another trick.

She rolls over and with two paws at the top of the mat and her back paws at the bottom of the mat, she rises on all fours with her body long and pushes up and down. That's when I jump on her back and make her body hit the floor. She acts like she doesn't want me to do this, but I know she loves it because she laughs every time.

🐾 🐾 🐾 🐾

*I take Mac on an hour-long walk every morning and play ball with him in the park each afternoon. I take him on my walks to Starbucks and the post office. For a city dog, that's a lot of exercise. But it's never enough for Mac. If I'm moving, he wants to move, too.*

*Each night, as I spread out my yoga mat on the bedroom floor, Mac assumes it's a welcome to fun time with Mary, or Twister for humans and dogs.*

*When I lay on my back to do sit-ups, he jumps on my tummy. When I roll over to do push-ups, he jumps on my back. I know I should make him behave and let me have some personal exercise time, but it's so funny, and he gets so excited that I can't help but make a game out of it.*

*I can't beat him, so I decide to let him join me. I lie flat on my back and grab one of his favorite toys. He stands between my legs as we play tug-of-war with my torso pulling back onto the floor and Mac pulling me to sit up. It's the closest thing to sit-ups I can do with Mac around.*

*When I stand in place and do arm circles that Shape Magazine recommends for tightening the flab where shoulders meet armpits, Mac stands on his hind legs and puts his front paws on my shoulders. I walk forward and he backs up, continuing to rest his paws on my shoulders. I walk backward and he moves with me.*

*A few more weeks and we'll be ready for "Dancing with the Dogs."*

## Going off the Deep End

Mary is angry at me, and she should be. She told me not to get in the pool. I understood what she said and she knew that I understood, but I did it anyway. I couldn't help it. I love the splash I make when my body hits the water. I love to swim. I love beating Sadie to the bobbing tennis ball in the middle of the pool. I love shaking the water off and hearing leashers squeal.

So here I am sitting with a shallow pool of water under my body, avoiding her stare as she points her finger at me and firmly states, "Bad dog."

Why do I defy her? I don't know. Maybe I have water in my ears. Maybe I'm a pool addict. Maybe it's because I know that Mary will still love me even when I disobey. Or, maybe I don't want to be a goody-four-paws.

🐾 🐾 🐾 🐾

*When Laura invited us to her pool, I jumped at the chance, and Mac jumped in the pool... and jumped and jumped. Since I don't have a pool, I often envision lounging poolside in a comfortable padded chair, throwing a tennis ball in the water with my two-foot purple "Chuck-It!" tennis ball launcher and basking in the expression on Mac's face as he retrieves and places the ball by my side.*

*But visions aren't reality, and the joy on Mac's face is the lone truth in this daydream. Psycho Mac crashes into the water to capture the launched tennis ball, hastily returns to within four inches of my chair, stops, and madly shakes his drenched body. Wet fur and three gallons of chlorinated water rain over me like an out-of-control water sprinkler, and no matter how much I brace myself, the ice-cold water sends chills down my spine and shocks my nervous system. He drops the rolling tennis ball just out of my reach so that I have to put down the soaked magazine I'm reading to scoop up the ball and experience this "ecstasy" all over again.*

*After 30 minutes of this irritating game, I summon Mac out of the pool. It takes three heavy beach towels to dry him off, limb by limb, ear by ear, tummy, back, and tail until he is moderately damp as opposed to soaking wet.*

*"Mac, no more pool," I command firmly.*

*I turn around to pick up the mountain of terrycloth only to see a blond ball of fur flying into the water. When he gets out, I grab him by the previously dry collar I'd just put on him and scream, "Lay down!"*

*He pulls his "I'm-not-going-to-look-in-her-eyes-because-I-know-she's-mad-at-me" game.*

*"Bad dog," I say sternly and repeatedly. Mac lays there shaking, looking in every direction but mine, and avoiding my reprimanding eye contact. It's hard for me to be mad at Mac, so I look away. I don't want to give in to his charms.*

*I love how happy Mac is when he gets to swim and play fetch in a pool. I know that it's great exercise for him, good for his joints, and wears him out for the rest of the day. I have to remember lounging and reading by a pool has to be a mutually exclusive event from taking Mac swimming. It's either all about him or all about me. Like many things in life, we can't always have it both ways.*

## Missing

I'm scared. Mary's not here. She fed me dinner early and left. Since she's been gone, it's turned dark and light again. I'm bored. I miss her a lot. She knows I don't like to stay by myself, so where is she? Has something bad happened to her? My mind races to lots of places and none of them good. Finally, I hear a key in the door.

I must be in shock because I don't jump up to welcome her home. I sit on the sofa like nothing unusual has happened. Mary throws her arms around my neck and mumbles through tears, "Baby, I am so sorry. I'll never leave you alone that long again." Well, let's hope not. I could have starved to death. And do you know how lucky you are that I can hold my pee all night? You could have had a real mess here. Mary, I was scared. This isn't like you. You're always here for me. Please keep your promise and never leave me alone like this ever again.

I relax now that she's home. I feel brave that I survived the night alone. By the looks of her, Mary didn't. Her hair is messed up and she is carrying the clothes that she left in. They smell like food from her stomach, like the chunky stuff on the sidewalk she pulls me away from on Sunday morning walks. She looks terrible.

Betty, a leasher with pink toenails, is with her. But she doesn't look bad like Mary. Betty's been staying with us for a few days and carries beef jerky in her purse, so she's alright by me.

I have to pee, bad. Betty takes me outside to do my business. I want Mary to go. Why isn't she taking me out? I go with Betty because I really have to go, but I go back in as soon as I pee.

When we get back in, Mary feeds me and then falls down on the couch. I don't like seeing Mary like this. I like it when she wakes up fresh and excited about the walk we're getting ready to take. Not like this, where she lies on the sofa and sends others to do the things we usually do together.

It wasn't fun when she was missing, and it's not that much better now. Mary moves from the bed to the sofa to the bed to the sofa. Even when she tries to pet me she sticks her finger in my eye because she's covered her face with a washcloth.

What's going on? I want my Mary back.

*I wake up in a stupor. I look around the room through the slits in my eyes and realize I'm in Rex's guest room. I look at my watch and it says 8:00. Since it's light outside, I deduce that it's morning. "Oh my God," I scream inside, and even the silent shriek hurts my head. Mac has been by himself for over twelve hours. I rarely leave him alone more than four.*

*I stumble into the living room to find Betty, my dear friend visiting from Virginia, standing in front of a mirror applying lipstick. I see my reflection beside hers and it's something lipstick won't help.*

*"I think I was over-served last night. Why are we here? What happened?"*

*"Well, let's see. After you threw up in a bush in front of the Abbey, we got in a cab and came here where you threw up again."*

*"Why did we come here? My place is closer."*

*"You and Rex discussed that, since we only had enough cash to make one stop. But then he gave this address to the taxi driver."*

*"Where's Rex?"*

*"In his room."*

*The door opens and our friend Tim walks in with Bella, a hyper 150-pound bloodhound. "Hey Mary, you left your dinner on the sidewalk. Bella enjoyed it," he says, laughing.*

*"Don't laugh so loud and give us a ride home, please. Mac's been by himself all night long."*

*I am a nervous wreck thinking about what I'll find at home. When I walk in the house, Mac is lying on the long orange chaise in his typical Sphinx position. He doesn't even jump down to greet me. I walk over and gave him a big hug.*

*"Baby, I am so sorry. I'll never leave you alone that long again."*

*The rest of the day is a waste, which is usually what follows a night of getting wasted. I'm mad at myself for spoiling Betty's visit and for leaving Mac by himself for so long.*

*If there is a silver lining in this pitcher of margaritas, it's that Mac is capable of staying by himself without incident. It's nice to know this, but I won't put it into practice. Just because he can be by himself all night doesn't mean he should.*

## An Only Child

I know what she's thinking. I can see it in her eyes when someone tells us about a stray dog. I hear it in her voice, in the questions she asks two-dog leashers. I see her looking at pictures of dogs in the back of magazines and on the square box on her desk.

I like other dogs. Sniffing them on daily walks gives me a break from lying on the couch. My friends at Hollywood Hounds Daycare are cool. But do I want another dog in the house for keeps? I don't think so.

UB, Toby, Sam, and I talked about this at school today.

UB is a small, white Shih Tzu that smiles all the time and has an unusual bark. He barks in threes, always. He sees a dog he doesn't like, "ruff, ruff, ruff." He wants a ball that's under the sofa, "ruff, ruff, ruff." It's time to eat, "ruff ruff, ruff."

UB is an only dog like me. Not like me, he had bad leashers before he had good ones. A nice lady found UB covered in oil in a big can. His bad leashers had left him there to die, so it's good the nice lady found him. But she didn't like his bark, so she asked two leashers named Aaron and Joe to keep him for a while. A while became forever, and Aaron and Joe became UB's leashers. That's why UB smiles all the time.

Toby and Sam are brother and sister. Sam sounds like a boy but is really a girl whose real name is Samantha. They didn't have the same mother or father, but they have the same leashers. Both are Labradoodles but look nothing alike.

Toby is tall and stately with curly sandy hair and looks more like a poodle than a Lab. He's got long legs, and Mary calls him a supermodel. Sam doesn't look like a Lab or a poodle. I think she is her own breed. She has the body of an overgrown dachshund with a small head and a pointy nose. She's got sweet eyes that give you no choice but to like her. She's got pretty fur when it's not falling out.

UB and I told Toby and Sam how great it is not to have to share your toys, food, or leashers. "We get to go more places because it's easier to take one dog than two," we argued.

"We are never alone because we have each other. So even when our leashers are gone, we still have company," Toby and Sam replied. "And it's fun to share toys. How do you play tug-of-war with yourself?"

UB and I looked at each other. Yeah, they may have a point. But I'll take Mary over sharing any time.

*I've struggled with Mac being an only dog. At times, I wish I had gotten two dogs when I got him. A sibling would keep him company when I'm gone and alleviate my guilt for leaving. Plus, I love seeing the bond between dogs in a two-dog family*

*It was the right thing for me (and him) at the time. I'd never had a dog before, so it made sense that I'd start with one. Mac likes other dogs, but he tires of them after a few butt sniffs. Whenever another dog comes to visit, Mac is elated when the guest leaves so he doesn't have to guard his toys and tennis balls. Mac is happier when he's the center of attention. He's jealous of other dogs that stay longer than their owners.*

*Our friends Mick and Lou have two Labradoodles who are physically and emotionally inseparable. They are not blood relatives, but Mick and Lou got Samantha (Sam) about two months after Toby, so they've been together all of Sam's life and most of Toby's.*

*They rarely leave each other's side except when forced. When Sam got sick and was in and out of the hospital, Toby was a wreck. His sleep was fitful and his waking hours were spent whining and looking around the house for Sam.*

*Sam became sluggish and her stomach was distended. She started losing her fur. Her body looked like the head of an elderly woman whose hair has* *fallen out, revealing her ashen scalp. Lou took Sam to the vet. First they thought it was allergies and prescribed meds accordingly. But Sam did not get better. After multiple tests, the vet determined Sam had Cushing's disease. Fortunately the disease is treatable with medicine. Unfortunately, it costs $150 a month for the rest of her life. But she's worth it. All dogs are worth it.*

*Expenses are a consideration when owning more than one dog. It's twice the cost of food, insurance, veterinarian and grooming bills, and daycare and overnight charges when you go out of town. Two dogs are best served by two incomes.*

*Another dog mama guilt I sometimes have is that I got Mac from a breeder when there are so many dogs in pounds that need to be rescued.*

*Aaron and Joe first fostered and then adopted a precious eight-pound white Shih Tzu named UB. Saving a dog from evil owners is in itself a noble act, but Aaron embellishes the rescue. The story goes, from Aaron's telling, that UB was found dripping in black oil in a tall can behind a gas station. His vocal cords had been cut, which explains his funny little bark. A passerby heard something moving in the can and rescued UB from near death.*

*It's too soon to say, and I hope I have another decade before I have to decide. But when Mac leaves this earth, I hope I'm in a position to adopt two dogs. After having Mac, I'm pretty sure I will always want to have a dog. And I'm certain it will take two dogs to provide the love I've found in one Mac.*

# I Am an Actor

*"I'd like to audition for Sleep, Eat, Play, Love"*

—Mac

## The Audition

Mary looked up from the morning paper and asked, "Mac, would you like to be an actor? I'm going to fill out an application for you." I looked at her with the expression I have when she uses words that I don't know, like "actor" or "application," but Mary was excited, so I shrugged and continued licking yesterday's bone. Three days later, Le PAWS (Pets at Work on Set) called to say they were holding an open casting call. They wanted to know if I could audition on Saturday.

I didn't give the matter much thought until Saturday came and instead of the long car ride ending at a dog park, it ended in a parking lot. There were lots of dogs and leashers I'd never seen before. A pretty girl in pink pants with skinny ankles took us to a room with other dogs and leashers. I waited patiently beside Mary since she had the choke collar on me and I didn't have much choice. I looked around the room at the nervous dogs and leashers. I wondered if I was at a new vet's office.

We hadn't been there long when Skinny Ankles called our name and led us down a narrow hallway. She seemed to be the alpha-leasher. I wanted to sniff the floor as we walked, but Mary had too tight a hold on me. Skinny Ankles led us into a large room and introduced us to Lucy and John. Lucy was taller than most leashers because my nose barely reached her knee. Just the opposite, John was short and round, a leasher version of a bulldog. John told Mary to remove my choke chain.

I liked these guys already.

I explored the room while John and Lucy talked to Mary. Mary called me, but I acted like I didn't hear her. There were too many new scents to sniff. Then came the all too familiar, "Mac, NOW!" and I knew she meant business. By this time, John was sitting at a desk away from the others.

Lucy handed Mary a handful of beef nuggets. I nudged Mary's closed fist to get what was obviously meant for me. But Mary stuck her non-nugget hand in my face and I knew I would have to earn the treats. Okay, I'll play that game. Lucy told Mary to tell me to sit, which I did and was immediately given a beef bit.

"Stay." I got another nugget. Easy.

"Down." Another easy one! I got a treat.

"Shake." Yawn, another treat. Wow, this is fun. I could do this all day with one paw tied behind my back. After each request, Lucy checked off a box on a sheet of paper attached to a clipboard.

Lucy then insulted my intelligence by asking Mary if I could catch a tennis ball. Mary threw the ball. I don't mean to brag, but I was impressive. Lucy asked Mary to sit down while Lucy gave me instructions. Normally, I don't leave Mary for someone I hardly know, but Mary was out of treats and Lucy had a handful.

Lucy led me around the room, gave me some commands, which I obeyed and was immediately rewarded. She walked me over to a bunch of tin cans hanging by strings from a board. She rattled the cans, which made a lot of noise, but I didn't care. I wanted the food. She got on the other side of the cans, and told me to walk toward her. Okay, I'll do what you want. Just give me the beef. She seemed pleased that I could walk through cans and told Mary that this test was to see how I reacted to loud noises. Like I said, who cares about cans rattling when there's a handful of meat to eat? After passing the noise test, Lucy sent me back to Mary's side while she and John looked at the clipboard and whispered to each other.

Lucy returned to us and announced that I had passed with flying colors and was hereby accepted into the Le PAWS Animal Actors Training Program. The door opened, Skinny Ankles returned, and escorted Mary and me to my agent's office. I wasn't sure what the big deal was or what an "agent" was, but Mary sure was excited. She told me I was going to be the next Old Yeller.

Old yellow what? I wondered.

*The ad in the Los Angeles Times read, "Would your dog like to be an actor? Auditions happening soon." If there were truth in advertising, it should have read, "Would you like for your dog to be an actor?" I never recall Mac, upon seeing a dog on television, come running to me begging, "Mary, I want to be in a dog food commercial. Please help me become an actor." But in celebrity-obsessed Los Angeles, people like being part of the industry, and I'm no different.*

*While I've never dreamed of being in a soap opera or seeing my face on a Sunset Strip billboard, I'm intrigued by the faces that don the front of People Magazine. Even if I aspired to stardom, the constant glare of the spotlight and flash of paparazzi cameras, the invasion of your privacy, and the nutcases that stalk today's celebrities would make me rethink that career choice. But being the mother of a Hollywood dog sounded quite fun to me. I could be around famous people but not be one. I left a voicemail, and two days later they invited Mac to their open casting call.*

*The audition consists of Lucy, a professional animal trainer, giving Mac a series of commands and John, the owner of Le PAWS, sitting in the corner of the room observing. My chest swells with pride as Mac performs each request Lucy gives him, thanks to the soft beefy treats he's awarded for each correct response. Lucy and John confer while counting checked boxes on a sheet of paper pinned to a clipboard Lucy holds. I sit patiently beside Mac, whispering in his ear how proud I am of him, no matter what the outcome.*

*Lucy and John break from their small huddle and Lucy announces, "Mac is very coachable and could be trained to be a studio dog."*

*I'm introduced to Cliff, Mac's agent. Cliff is tall, good looking, likable and not pushy like Hollywood agents are often portrayed. He explains the training program, owner responsibilities, costs and process for getting Mac into print, television, and movies.*

*There's an eight-week training for the two of us followed by a canine good citizenship test and then we're on our way to doggy stardom. Visions of Mac on the big screen dance in my head. But first I have to cut a check for $1,200, which at the time seemed little to pay for the opportunity to be a Hollywood Mom for a modern-day Old Yeller.*

## Acting School

"Today's the day," Mary coos to me after breakfast and a walk. "You have an acting lesson." The last time she said "acting," I got lots of treats, so I jump in the car. After a long drive, we pull into the parking lot of Le PAWS. Skinny Ankles is there and so is Lucy, the beef-log leasher. We go into a big room where, based on the carpet, many dogs have been before. Other actors are there, but I'm the only Lab.

There are two Great Danes named Conan and Capone. I don't remember which is which, although they look nothing alike. Conan, or is it Capone, is white with black spots. He looks like a Dalmatian on steroids. He has one blue eye and one brown eye and reminds me of a big stuffed animal. Every time I look at him, I want to tear his eyes out and find his squeaker. Not a good idea, since he probably weighs twice as much as I do. The other Great Dane is brown and black like a shepherd. Both of his eyes are brown. There is an old golden retriever named Jack with gray fur on his face who seems content with life. I want to smell and play with the others, but Beef Log Lucy won't let me. Every time we try to get together, Lucy barks at our leashers to make us stay in our own part of the room.

I realize Lucy is the leader and if I expect to get any treats, I have to do what she says. Lucy gives each leasher a small red toy called a *clicker*. I sniff Mary's clicker to see if it's something to eat, but it's not.

Lucy calls me to the front of the room. I can smell the treats in her hand, but she won't give me any. She tells me to sit. I sit. Just as I sit, she clicks her clicker and I get a treat. She tells me to lay down. I lay down, she clicks, and I get a treat.

Then Mary takes over. Sit, click, treat. Down, click, treat. This is fun, I love clickers! I would have done this all day, but Lucy makes Mary stop clicking and take me back to my spot in the room. I sit there while, one-by-one, Conan, Capone, Jack, and all the others play the clicking game with Lucy and their leashers.

After every dog has a turn, we leave the big room and go outside. The leashers let us smell each other… finally. I pee on a rose bush and jump in the car. I think about my day. I like going to Le PAWS. I need to listen to Lucy since she always has treats. It's hard to sit still while other dogs get treats. I like clickers.

I hear the garage door open. I don't remember the drive home. I'm still half asleep when I jump out of the car. Wow, I'm tired. Like I've been chasing balls for an hour. Acting is intense, but I sure do like the attention.

*Can competition and genuine support co-exist in the DNA of a Hollywood Mom? Today is the first of eight consecutive Saturdays of training for Mac to become a working actor. Lucy, the studio trainer we met last week, asks for a volunteer. I raise Mac's paw. She attaches an eight-foot leash to Mac and hands me a clicker. Lucy says, "Mac, sit." He sits, she clicks, and gives him a treat. She tells me to do it.*

*"Mac, sit." He does, I click, and give him a treat. I'm proud.*

*"Have him sit and stay. Walk to the far wall, count to 10, and get him to come to you." He does, I click, and give him a treat. I'm proud.*

*"Tell him to speak."*

*I say, "Mac, speak." Mac barks, I click, and give him a treat. I'm beaming with pride.*

*"Good job. Now make him roll over." I have Mac sit and move the treat over his body in a circular motion. He jumps up to grab the treat. No click, no treat. I try again. Mac lunges at the clicker as if clicking it himself will result in the desired reward.*

*Okay, three out of four's not bad. We return to our section of the room.*

One by one, Lucy calls the others to the front of the room and gives similar instructions. Outwardly, I join the Hollywood moms and dads shouting encouraging remarks and showering compliments for achieved obedience. On the inside, I secretly hope the competitors are unable to follow instructions.

I realize this is wasted jealousy, since a two-foot-tall, eighty-five-pound Lab, a six-inch-tall, four-pound Yorkie, and a four-foot, hundred-pound Great Dane would unlikely vie for the same part—like sending Sidney Portier, Dustin Hoffman, and Jack Black to the same audition. But common sense doesn't reign in this critical moment in Mac's career. Mac, with his baritone bark, is the only one that can speak on cue.

He's sure to be the Sidney Portier of the dog world.

## First Role

*It was the hardest $80 I ever made. Mac's agent called and asked if Mac was available the following day to play the family dog on an episode of* Life, *a cop drama in its second season. He would be photographed with his make-believe family and used for live scenes as well.*

*I followed Le PAWS' explicit on-the-set directions to the letter. I packed Mac's suitcase with his headshots, vaccination records, doggy treats, hand wipes, water bowl and beach towel for him to lie on. The morning of, I loaded Mac and gear into the SUV before sunrise to make our 7:00 a.m. call time in the 100-degree San Fernando Valley. We beat the traffic, but not the heat.*

*The episode was being shot "on location" as opposed to a studio set, which in this case was a modest ranch-style home in a middle-class neighborhood.*

*When shooting on location, studios set up a "base camp" where trailers for the "talent," producers, directors, wardrobe, etc., park until shooting is finished. When we arrived at base camp, a production assistant (P.A. in the world of entertainment) told me, "They want you in Makeup."*

*"Uhh, I'm here for my dog, Mac. Do I need makeup?"*

*"The director wants to see how Makeup does a black eye for a future scene. You'll get a bump."*

*This is the first of the Hollywood extra lingo I learned that day. Extras on the set of a movie or television show get paid a set rate for eight hours. If you are asked to do anything out of the ordinary, you get a bump in pay. Have a dog, get a bump. Cut your hair, get a bump. Use your car, get a bump. Get a black eye, get a bump.*

*And so I got a black eye—a very effective one. It looked like I'd caught a major league pitch using my eye socket for a baseball glove. It was black, yellow, purple, and puffy. After he was finished beating me up with eye shadow and eyeliner, Tex (the makeup artist), Mac, and I rode in a van to the house where the show was taping. Mac stared at my black eye with concern. I smiled and rubbed him behind his ears to assure him I was okay.*

*We pulled up to a suburban, white, ranch-style house. Tex and I made our way through the multitude of people and equipment to see the director who took one look at me.*

*"I want it puffier."*

*We got back in the van and returned to the makeup trailer where Tex wacked me harder with a makeup bat to give me a real shiner. Back on set, the director couldn't be interrupted to check my mess of an eye, which worked out fine since it was time for Mac to take center stage, or at least center of the dusty garage where his family portrait was to be shot.*

*On the way to "Action," Mac had a little action of his own. As I untied him from the tree where he was waiting patiently, Mac took one step, threw his butt to the ground, and crapped a mountain.*

*Welcome to Hollywood.*

*I looked up from my bagging to apologize to the P.A. in charge of the shoot but gratefully she was ten steps ahead of us, never realizing stage fright had struck the family dog in a bad way.*

*Grinning from relief, Mac's performance as the family dog was stellar. Energized by the rush of the camera, we could hardly wait until his next scene. But wait we did, for the next five hours in the hot Valley sun, never to be called for another scene.*

*By the time we were released, I was soaked in sweat and the makeup from my fake black eye was sliding down my face and quickly approaching my neck. Mac, panting from the heat, exhausted from his marathon day in the sun, fell asleep the moment his paws hit the car seat.*

*Months later, we witnessed the fruits of Mac's labor. The lead character, Charlie, walks into his ex-partner Brent's house for the first time in more in than a decade. During Charlie's twelve years in jail,*

*Brent married, had two children, bought a house, and moved to the Valley. As Brent leaves to put Charlie's host gift on ice, Charlie stares at the idyllic family portrait in the foyer, complete with the family dog. The camera zooms in on Mac and his Hollywood family for five dramatic minutes—provided you hit the pause button.*

## Mr. October

I'm not only an actor. I'm also a model. You probably remember me best as Mr. October 2008 in the "Just Labs" calendar. And when it says, "Just Labs," it means just Labs. There are no leashers in the shot, no trees, no ocean—just a Lab and a white background. Some months have more than one Lab. February, for example, is three Labs—yellow, chocolate, and black—standing side-by-side looking up in the same direction. The cover is a litter of Lab puppies. Puppies sell calendars. But I rule October with my up-close profile and a ball in my mouth. That was my idea.

As famous as this calendar is, it almost didn't happen. When we got to the photo shoot, they sent Mary away. I was having none of this and refused to cooperate. A small leasher with a small voice gave me commands. I could hardly hear her so I pretended not to.

Then Mary walked back into the room. I was happy again. My leasher was here. But they told her to sit in the corner of the room and watch. Again, not what I wanted, so I made little effort to do what they asked until they let Mary play.

No one puts Mr. October's leasher in the corner.

*Mac's agent called to see if he would be available for a photo shoot for a Labs-only calendar. It wasn't a paying role, but it would be good for his portfolio. When we arrived at the studio, I was told there was a dog trainer on the shoot and I could wait in the lounge or outside on the patio. It shouldn't take long. Or so they thought.*

*I had just settled down in a big wicker rocker with a fluffy floral pad and pillow when I heard, "Are you Mac's Mom?"*

*"Yes, is anything wrong?"*

*"He keeps looking for you. Come into the studio and hopefully he will calm down."*

*I followed the assistant down a long hall and into the room where they were shooting. Mac came to me, running in circles around my legs, howling, and licking my face as if we'd been separated for months as opposed to minutes. After the overly dramatic reunion, I sat in the corner of the room as I was told, praying for Mac to calm down and follow directions.*

*He did, but continued to look for me out of the corner of his eye. The trainer, timid and soft-spoken, could not hold his attention. Not wanting to be one of those Hollywood Moms who interrupts the artistic process, I sat still and kept my mouth shut until I could stand it no more.*

*"Would you like me to give the commands?" I asked. With nothing to lose, they allowed me to communicate the photographer's vision to my supermodel-in-training. Under my direction, Mac sat where he was supposed to and moved and looked where he was told.*

*Now that Mac was performing like a true professional under my effective tutelage, I deemed it acceptable to provide creative input and suggested Mac be photographed with a tennis ball. I could almost see him wink at me when the photographer agreed.*

*The day's events slipped my mind until 18 months later while browsing the aisles at Bed Bath & Beyond. A calendar with six adorable Lab puppies caught my eye. I turned the calendar over to see my baby, ball in mouth, owning October.*

*The next day, every Bed Bath & Beyond store in Los Angeles was sold out of the "Just Labs" calendar.*

## Lights, Camera, Action

Acting is harder than it looks. Today, I shoot an episode of *Criminal Minds*. This time Mary gets to be on the show, too. I like that.

Unlike the last television show I shot on location, we're not allowed to park at base camp. We have to park in a big empty lot and wait for someone to pick us up. Henry, the nice driver, helps Mary get me and all her bags into the van.

We're greeted at base camp by a girl in jeans with holes in them carrying a clipboard. "Are you Mary?" she asks.

Mary replies, "Yes."

"You need to go to wardrobe in the last trailer on the left. Ask for Nicky." Nicky is nice but she doesn't like what Mary is wearing. She gives her clothes and tells her to change in the next trailer.

It's cool inside and I don't want to leave. But Mary says we have to go back to Nicky so she could see if Mary's outfit looks right. I thought her other outfit was fine. Nicky says, "That's better. You can go to the set."

We get back in the van and Henry drops us off on a street with trees and houses, my kind of place. There are more trailers and lots of leashers. Many are standing around doing nothing while others walk quickly from place to place talking into little black boxes with cords hanging from their ears. Some are standing by themselves reading a big stack of papers, talking into the air. Leashers are telling other leashers what to do.

There's a lot going on, but most of the leashers stop to pet me no matter how much of a hurry they're in. There are men on carts with big equipment following some of the other people around. A big man in a baseball cap yells, "Action!" Some people start moving and talking while others stand deathly still until the big guy yells, "Cut!" I guess he's the pack leader.

A guy named Josh in shorts, with pictures on his leg, tells us to wait in a big tent. It's quiet there and I get to rest. It's 9:30 in the morning and so much has already happened. I'm not used to this pace.

My nap is interrupted by a girl with one of the cords in her ear. "Hi, I'm Melissa. They're ready for you." Mary and I have to walk fast to keep up with Melissa's long legs. Melissa introduces us to the pack leader whose name is Coach. Coach is cool. Although Coach is big and aggressive, he is likable and caring, like a Greater Swiss Mountain dog.

"Stand here," Coach says. "When I say 'rolling,' walk toward the camera. When you hear a car skid, turn around and look."

Our job seems easy enough, and it is… the first twenty times. Mary and I always do our parts right, but the other actors can't seem to get their parts right. Coach tells us to break for lunch and come back after we've eaten. Lunch, eat—I like this Coach guy even if he's picky about our scene.

During lunch, we sit under a big tree and talk to a pretty girl with kind eyes. Her job is to stand in for another person on the show. I don't know why they call it a "stand-in," because she sits around a lot. I think she'd rather be standing, but that decision is up to Coach. I was right about him being the pack leader. I'm enjoying attention from Kind Eyes and the other stand-ins when Melissa yells for us.

"Mary and Mac, they're ready for you." So back to our street corner we go to do the scene over again. Sometimes we have to walk, turn and look when Coach yells, "Action!" Other times, we can sit down but not leave our street corner.

We sit without walking for a long time. Mary asks Coach if we can leave our spot to get me some water. Coach looks at my tongue hanging out of my mouth and says, "Sure." I lap up a bottle of water so quickly that Mary pours another. Then Melissa tells us we're wrapped. Wrapped in what?

We repeat our morning in reverse. We get in a van, return to base camp, Mary puts on her own clothes and we get in a van that returns to the parking lot where we began our day, which seems like a month ago. I sleep all the way home.

I think I need a stand-in.

## Leading Lady

Her name is Craft Services. My pet name for her is Crafty. I am not allowed near her, so I admire her beauty and sniff her scent from afar.

Crafty is a trailer with big windows on the side that flip up. Two men in white hats are inside making food. Milk pours from a pipe attached to Crafty's belly. She has rows of hot food, like eggs and bacon and gravy and bread. Another shelf has cold food, like yogurt and fruit. I'm not about to choose that when gravy's around.

The men in white hats put baskets of cheese, candy, beef logs, nuts, and cereal on the tables outside the trailer. Round tubs of ice sit under the table with bobbing water bottles and soda cans.

Mary knows I want to be with Crafty. She keeps us apart by tying me to a tree just out of Crafty's reach. This isn't fair. Crafty has food to give. I want food. We belong together.

*There it is, my nemesis, Craft Services. All day long, the evil trailer stocks my favorite foods, calling my name, tempting me with baskets of colorful M&M's and mixed nuts, sans peanuts. Miniature candy bars boast their brands through glass bowls. Peanut butter and chocolate granola bars disguise themselves as healthy alternatives.*

*In the morning, Krispy Kreme donuts jump from an open red, white, and green box into my line of sight. Steam rises from hot plates of gravy and biscuits. It's ironic that one of the few places in L.A. that serves white gravy with chunks of sausage is a transportable kitchen in the land of actresses who eat lettuce and a Tic Tac for lunch.*

*Mid-day, Craft Services moves beyond the confines of a trailer to a tent of steamer trays filled with fried and barbecued chicken, pork ribs, and fish in a cream sauce. Macaroni and cheese, mashed potatoes, and French fries* are available so no one's desired starch is left out. The dessert table looks like the Mother's Day buffet at Marie Callender's. There's also a salad bar so the actresses don't have to pack a lunch.

Around 4:00 p.m., because it's been almost three hours since a meal was served, pizza arrives along with breadsticks. The aroma of chocolate chip cookies baking in the background fills the air.

What extras don't receive in salary is made up for in calories.

## A Sunsetting Career

*The turning point in Mac's acting career came when he was hired for a print ad for a pharmaceutical company. The backdrop for the photo shoot was a brick courtyard behind The Culver Hotel, a historic boutique hotel established in 1924 in Culver City, California.*

*We arrived early for our 7:00 a.m. call time and walked to Starbucks for a latte until it was time to find Kate, the producer of the shoot. Kate was a dog lover and took instantly to Mac who sat and listened intently to his instructions for the day. Kate introduced us to Maya, a beautiful, tall, thin, dark-skinned model dressed in cropped gray Lycra yoga pants, a grey and yellow sports bra, and running shoes. Maya, Mac's costar for the day, acknowledged Mac but didn't seem thrilled to be working with a dog. Kate walked us over to a roped-off area where a three-man crew was untangling cords, arranging lights, and setting up multiple tripods. There we met Jake, the director, and Taylor, the photographer.*

*The job was straightforward. When Jake yelled "Action!" Maya and Mac were to walk calmly from left to right while Taylor photographed their journey. The problem was that Mac refused to walk across the courtyard with Maya. He would take a few steps and once he realized I wasn't coming with them, he pulled her back in my direction.*

*Then the director had an idea that he thought would work for all the models on set. I was instructed to stand outside the view of the camera on the right. Maya, with Mac at her side, would be left of the camera. When he yelled "Action!" Mac would walk with Maya since I would be waiting for him on the other side. The trick worked, but Mac was so anxious to get to me that he practically ran across the courtyard with Maya in tow. Take two was the same as the first, if not faster. The attractive model who thought her day would consist of sashaying across a cobblestone piazza had to practically run to keep up with the four-legged model who had taken over the set.*

*The director paused the action to check the film. My stomach was in* knots because Mac was not doing what he was supposed to do. My anxiety diminished when I saw Jake and Taylor pointing to the lens and smiling as they reviewed the takes. To the delight of everyone but Maya, Jake liked that the camera captured movement and changed the shoot to have Maya run, not walk, across the courtyard with Mac.

When the shoot was over, Mac and I returned to the mobile trailer that served as Kate's temporary office. Unlike other gigs, Mac was paid cash for his work. Also unlike other jobs, Mac received a report card that would be shared with his agent. The knots in my stomach returned, but Kate was more than kind. Mac and I received good marks for being on time, for his cleanliness, and for my preparedness with treats, leashes, and collars as requested. One "constructive" comment was that Mac experienced some separation anxiety. SOME? Yes, Kate took it easy on us.

It wasn't Mac's last acting or modeling gig, but it was the beginning of more scrutiny of the jobs we did accept. If I couldn't be in the scene with him or wasn't the one giving him instructions, I turned down the job.

This role made me realize that Mac becoming a star for the world to see was much less important than me being a star in his eyes.

# Fun and Whimsy

*"Drinking raindrops; kittens who don't run;
treats and tennis balls not tied by a string;
these are a few of my favorite things."*

—Mac

## The Way You

*I love the way you lay.*
*I love the way you play.*
*I love the way you kiss*
*And the way you miss*
*Me when I'm gone.*

*I love the way you smell*
*When you've just had a bath*
*I love the way you seem to laugh*
*While you wait for me*
*To throw you a ball.*

*I love your tail,*
*The way you swish it when you walk.*
*I love the way it goes in circles*
*When you're excited to see me.*

*I love to watch you run*
*Because you have so much fun*
*Chasing a dirty tennis ball*
*As if someone else would want it.*

# MAN OF THE HOUSE

*I love the way you cuddle.*
*I love the way you snuggle.*
*I love the warmth you bring to my bed*
*When it's cold outside.*

*I love the way you dive into the waves*
*And come out spitting*
*To get the salt off your tongue,*
*Just to go back for more.*

*I love the way you get excited*
*When you see a dog you know.*
*I love how you crouch on the sidewalk*
*So you don't scare little dogs.*

*I love the way you speak*
*To people you haven't seen in a while.*
*As if you are saying,*
*"Where in the hell have you been?*
*Did you forget about me?*
*Don't let it happen again."*

*I love the look in your eyes*
*When you realize*
*That you're going in the car, too,*
*And don't have to stay home alone.*

*I love the way you stare at me*
*As if I were the messiah*
*Waiting for me to give you a sign*
*That you can eat your dinner.*

*I love to watch you sleep,*
*All curled in a ball.*
*I squeeze my arms around you,*
*Lay my head on your soft torso*
*And listen to your heart beat.*

*I love you Mac.*

## Ode to My Lover

I think about you all the time. I love the way your fuzzy skin feels against my tongue. I love you when your hair is clean and blonde. I love you just as much when you're covered with mud.

I love playing with you, whether we're rolling in the grass or jumping on the sidewalk. Whenever you are out of my sight, I look for you constantly—hiding behind a tree, under the sofa, anywhere we've played together.

I love searching for you among the flowers and leaves of life. The better you hide, the longer it takes to find you, and the sweeter it is when you're in my paws again.

When anyone else holds you, I go mad. I don't want to share you. I have to have you. I hover until you're back with me. I love you and all your nicknames: Penn, Wilson, and Dunlop.

I love your family. The two siblings you hang out with in that plastic can and your extended family that lives in the bucket in the closet. I get angry when people abuse you, hitting you back and forth across a net, each trying to hit you harder than the other.

People ask if I ever tire of you.

Never!

I want to hold you, caress you, and keep you safe under my paw. I would rather be with you than eat, than sleep, than breathe. Without you, I am nothing. I am a court without a net, a racket without a string.

I'm a boring game whose only score is love.

## Dream Weaver

I had the weirdest dream last night. I was running along the ocean and every time I took a step, sparkling yellow neon tennis balls jumped out of the water. I was in dog heaven trying to decide which one to chase first. Mary was beside me laughing wildly because she's happy when I'm happy.

I came to a big pile of rocks and the balls disappeared—and so did Mary. I was scared because she never leaves me alone at the beach. I didn't know what to do. I looked down the beach toward a row of big houses, but she wasn't there. I know she didn't go in the ocean, so the only option left was to climb over the rocks in front of me.

When I got to the other side, Mary was lying on her back in the sand with tennis balls attached to every part of her body. There were tennis balls in each eye socket, one stuck to her nose, one in her mouth, each ear, and her belly button. There were ten tennis balls on her fingers and ten on her toes.

I laughed so hard at the human tennis ball rack in front of me. I started licking the tennis balls off her body and she giggled because it tickled when I did that. By the time all the balls were off, she was laughing so hard she was crying. We sat there in the sand in a circle of tennis balls, laughing like a kid and a puppy.

Then, as if things weren't weird enough, it started raining. But it wasn't water falling from the sky. It was little pieces of beef kibbles. I looked up to see where the goodies were coming from, and there was a black and white cow flying overhead dropping treats from a big feed bucket. When the cow saw me looking at her, she winked and mooed.

Then I heard a clucking sound. Behind the flying cow was a chicken in a little red wagon. The chicken was wearing white gloves. As she started removing the gloves, one claw at a time, she threw chicken fingers down to me.

After the flying farm animal parade passed, I looked around and we were encircled by fifty dogs with their backs toward us. I jumped up and started going around the circle, smelling one butt at a time. That's when I woke up. Mary was staring wide-eyed at me.

"What were you dreaming about, Boo Bear?" she asked. "You were making funny sounds and sniffing and licking in your sleep." I smiled as I laid my head on the pillow, remembering where I was before I woke up.

I've never had such a crazy dream. I wonder if it had anything to do with eating those funny-looking cigarette butts before I went to bed, the ones that the long-haired kid next door throws in the bushes when he hears his mom open the door.

## Pee Instructions

1.  Detect smell.
2.  Interrupt a perfectly good walk to drag leasher over to azalea bush.
3.  Smell low where Homer went.
4.  Smell high where Nike went.
5.  Smell to the left where an unknown dog went.
6.  Decide this is not the bush you want.
7.  Pull leasher back onto sidewalk.
8.  Resume walk.
9.  Feel magnetic pull to a large pile of poop. Leasher resists.
10. Walk on.
11. Spy mattress on sidewalk.
12. Smell for canine and human scents.
13. Remember that favorite tree is ahead.
14. Pull leasher to said tree.
15. Smell tree while facing north.
16. Turn, smell tree while facing south.
17. Lift leg.
18. See Clyde coming down his steps.
19. Decide that peeing can wait.
20. Run over and smell Clyde's butt.
21. Act uninterested while Clyde smells mine.
22. Pull leasher in Clyde's direction.
23. Wait and pretend not to watch while Clyde pees.
24. Stand over spot where Clyde pees.
25. Lift leg.
26. Pee where Clyde peed.

Everything's more fun when you do it with a friend.

## What My Leasher Means to Me

Loving human

Everlasting friend

Always comes back to me

Speaks to me in a silly voice

Happy when I'm around

Enjoys walking and playing ball together

Remembers to say "I love you Mac" every night

# Transitions

*"The only thing constant in life is change."*

—François de la Rochefoucauld, author

## Change

Things have changed. Our morning walks are short. Our night walks are long. I spend more time with my friends at Hollywood Hounds than I do with Mary. I don't like it this way.

A noisy box wakes Mary up in the morning. Sometimes the noise goes on a long time before she hits a button to make the noise stop. She gets out of bed without scratching my tummy before she gets in the shower. Sometimes she doesn't even ask how my night was. She is always in a hurry.

Mary dresses different now. She puts on taller shoes. She doesn't let me rub up against her, and when I do, she pulls out a sticky white stick and rolls it over her body.

She never comes to pick me up at Hollywood Hounds any more. Frank, the head leasher, brings me home to an empty house and an empty bowl.

*The day I secretly prayed would never come came. The joys of being an entrepreneur and stay-at-home dog Mom did not materialize into an income that would allow me to continue. When the financial stress outweighed the freedom of working independently, I hit the job market. Gratefully, I beat the odds of the reported unemployment figures. After a series of interviews, I put on my corporate panties and went back to work.*

*On a typical day, I leave by 8:00 a.m. and am rarely home before 7:00 p.m. It's quite a culture shock for Mac, who was used to being with me 24/7. As I leave for work, Mac has cradled his three-foot-long body under the two-by-two-foot end table. I think it mimics the security of his childhood kennel. I kiss him goodbye on the bridge of his nose. He rarely looks at me, which is okay since it allows me to avoid the sadness in his eyes. On work days that require evening obligations, I take Mac to daycare. I wish I could afford this luxury every day so Mac wouldn't be home alone.*

*This transition is hard for me. I throw myself into a job that I'm grateful for, even though I'd rather be elsewhere. I try to maintain a positive attitude, which is much harder than the work requirements of a stressful job.*

*Like Mac's position under the end table, some days I want to crawl under my desk and avoid the stares of my profession.*

## Dude

*My dog is a dude. He has become a dog that every dog loves, but he doesn't give them the time of day. It's not that he thinks he's better than everyone else. He doesn't think about it at all.*

*Tahla, the sweetest Boxer I've ever met, loves Mac. Perhaps she's a cougar dog since she is seven years older than Mac. Tahla doesn't see out of one eye and the other is cataract-ridden. But she can spot Mac a block away. She runs to him and slides her body beside his. Getting no response, she smells the ground where he is sniffing, pretending to be interested in what he's interested in just to be near him.*

*Dogs at the park run along the fence we walk by to get into the dog park, barking at Mac, excited that in forty steps, he'll be inside with them. They crowd each other like groupies at a rock concert to see who can get to him first. Sometimes he might let them sniff him or, if they're the chosen one, he will smell them. But most of the time he shoves them aside to stand in the middle of the park, silently demanding I throw the ball.*

*He didn't used to be this way. He was the one who ran up to other dogs and initiated playtime. He was the one who got down on the sidewalk waiting for a dog he saw in the distance to approach. He was the dog that pulled me across the street like the tail of a kite to catch up to a dog walking in the other direction.*

*What's changed? I suppose it could be age or maturity. But I'd like to think it's the desire to live life differently, to try to be a different animal than he used to be.*

*I'm unsure at this point whether I'm talking about Mac or myself.*

*When I moved to Los Angeles, I was a social animal. Weekends started on Thursday night and Friday night became Saturday morning before I made it home. Living by the motto, "You can rest when you're dead," I slept a little, went to the gym before meeting a bunch of friends for a late breakfast at Fiddlers, a local favorite that served the best pancakes in Los*

*Angeles. Sunday supper with the group was tradition after an afternoon of margaritas at Marix, the popular Mexican restaurant that rolled back the roof every Sunday afternoon.*

*Now a typical weekend is a long walk with Mac after work on Friday, usually culminating at the yogurt shop. On Saturday, I get my nails done while Mac is at the groomer. Saturday night is dinner with friends and their dogs, and on Sunday, church with Mac in the morning and movie night at home to end the weekend.*

*Mac's become a dude, and together we're an old married couple.*

## Noisy Food

"GRR... GRR... GRR... GRR... GRR...."

Morning and night I hear it. I hate it. The sound hurts my ears. It means there will be no yummy smells. No plates to lick.

Mary doesn't have food any more, which means I don't either, except for the limited portion of kibbles she puts into my bowl.

For her breakfast and supper, Mary opens the cabinet. Takes out a big tub. Scoops powder from the tub into a cup. Adds water and ice. And then it begins.

"GRR... GRR... GRR...GRR... GRR...."

The sound goes on for a long time before Mary stops the machine making the noise. She removes the cup from the machine and sticks a straw in the milky contents. A few slurps and the thing that used to be called a meal is over.

"GRR... GRR... GRR... GRR... GRR...."

That's not the machine talking this time!

*My most recent effort to lose the twenty-plus pounds I gained since returning to full-time work involves substituting two meals a day with organic high-protein shakes, along with a nutritional cleanse that detoxifies your whole body.*

*Based upon the success of a dear friend, I order a thirty-day supply of nutritional shakes, juices, and snacks with instructions to eat one healthy meal a day, along with two healthy snacks. The other two meals are shakes, so I finally make good use of the Nutri-Bullet that has sat idle on my countertop for months. This is the suggested regimen for five days a week. The other two days are reserved for deep cleanses.*

*I like my new eating plan. The shakes are good, and I'm surprised at how much energy I have after I've cleansed. I am more particular about the real meal I eat. It's an easy plan. I save money by not going to the grocery store, and I don't have to cook. The numbers on the scale have not dropped significantly, but I definitely feel better.*

*Unfortunately for Mac, my daily healthy meal is typically at lunch with clients or at one of my favorite restaurants near the office. He no longer gets a portion of my dinner, pried away from me with big brown eyes.*

*I tell him that I'll have more energy to take him on more walks when I've lost weight, that I'll be a happier person and a better mom. I can tell he's not buying my reasoning.*

*He prefers leftover chicken.*

## Nanny Nate

I've been through a lot of changes lately. I don't like change. First Mary started leaving me alone all day long. Except for the days that I went to school. Then my school closed down and I was alone again every day.

Until Nate.

One day after my school closed, I was lying on the couch being lonely and sad. I heard footsteps on the sidewalk and keys in the front door. I barked loudly because they weren't Mary's footsteps or keychain. I was scared but tried to sound threatening. I ran to the door barking my head off to head off the intruder.

The door opened slowly and in walked Nate, Sammy, and Deuce. My fast-beating heart jumped for joy as happiness replaced fear.

Nate and Sammy are our next-door neighbors. Nate is a gray-topped leasher with strong legs who often has treats in his pockets. Sammy is a pug, about my age. Deuce is a smaller, younger pug who lives on Harper, one street over from Havenhurst.

"Come on Mac," said Nate. "You're going with us."

Oh boy! "Going with" is so much better than being home without Mary. I ran out the door before Nate could change his mind. Nate took Sammy, Deuce, and me to the park to do our business. Then we went to Nate's house.

Nate and Sammy have a big patio. It's a magical place. There are lots of places to lie around. There's a big bed in the shade when the weather is hot. There are large stuffed chairs in the sun when the weather is cool. There are lots of plants so you feel like you're outside but you don't have to be on a leash.

Sammy and I like to relax and chill. Deuce tries to get us to play. We humor him with a few runs around the patio chasing a tennis ball. Then we force him to play our game, chasing the sun from lounge chair to lounge chair.

Life is good again. I'm not home alone any more.

When the sun starts to go down, Nate calls me inside for supper. Not long after that, Deuce's leasher picks him up so it's just Nate, Sammy, and me. We lie on Nate's bed and watch sports, just us guys.

I hear familiar footsteps on the stairs outside and a knock on the door. It's my sweet Mary coming to take me home. I jump for joy, partly because she's here and partly to thank her for giving me Nate.

Dogs aren't meant to be alone.

*I'm not good with change. And another one was on its way.*

*Mac's daycare, Hollywood Hounds, was closing its doors. New owners were taking over the property and remodeling the space for a doggy daycare, but in the meantime, Mac was home alone again.*

*Then came "Nanny Nate" to the rescue!*

*Nate lives next door and has a precious pug named Sammy. Nate knew about our predicament and offered to pick Mac up in the afternoons and keep him until I got home. "He's no trouble at all," Nate said. "He can hang out with Sammy."*

*I don't think I realized how much I stressed about Mac being home alone until he wasn't. For the first time since I'd been back at work, I didn't have to hurry up and finish what I was doing or not finish at all. Even when Mac was at daycare, Hollywood Hounds closed at 6:00 and I either had to rush home or, more often than not, the owner brought Mac home to an empty house.*

*When I pick Mac up at Nate's, he barks and jumps and is happy to see me, but it's not that frantic barking that elicits sadness and guilt.*

*Like so many changes I often fear and dread, this one turned out to be good. Mac got a nanny, and the neighborhood got a brand-new doggy daycare named Posh Pets whose owners created a thriving beautiful business where Mac gets bathed by wonderful groomers and enjoys a plentiful selection of fun and healthy doggy treats.*

*Change can be good.*

## Ember's Lesson

*Life can turn on a dime.*

I had been out of town for a week, visiting Mom in Virginia. I love time with relatives but when I'm there, I miss Mac.

I was so happy to be home, and Mac and I were taking our morning walk. It was Friday, and we had the weekend before us. As we passed an apartment building four doors down, I saw Ben and Brenda walking slowly down the sidewalk with Ember lagging behind. I stopped dead in my tracks.

"What is wrong with Ember?"

Ember is a sweet, loving, goofy glob of love. She's a large, sturdy brown Doberman with tan markings and is the happiest, most playful dog on the street. Ember loves every dog and human, and we all love her back. This dog in front of me is a shadow of the Ember I know.

One eye was covered in mucus, unable to focus. Her robust uncoordinated pounce was replaced by slow careful steps taken only after a gentle pull of her leash. She didn't acknowledge Mac or me. Standing took all her energy.

"We were hoping someone else would tell you so we wouldn't have to," Ben replied.

We stood for a moment in silence before Brenda continued. "She was fine 12 days ago. Her body is full of cancer. We've been to several specialists, and there is nothing that can be done. Every time we go to a new doctor, the techs look at the X-rays and then at us with sympathy."

We cried and hugged and hugged and cried.

"We've made the whole neighborhood cry," said Brenda. "No one can believe how fast this has happened."

I hugged Ben and Brenda and leaned down to hug Ember for what would be the last time.

I didn't ask how long she had. I wanted to ask, but didn't want Ben and Brenda to have to tell me. I knew it couldn't be long. I saw Ben and

*Brenda on Friday. They lost their baby Saturday night.*

*The dog lovers on Havenhurst are in shock. One of our own has been taken from us when we didn't see it coming. Some didn't know she was sick until after she was gone. No matter when we found out, we all hugged our dogs a little longer and a little tighter because of her.*

*I think about Ember a lot. When I see Ben and Brenda walking down the street, a part of them is missing.*

*But what is missing is a gift for what is here. Life is short, and we never know if the end is just around the corner, so enjoy every day, doing what you love, and loving what you do. Be goofy. Have fun. Be nice to people and dogs, expecting nothing in return. Run and jump and tell your family you love them every time you see them.*

*Be Ember.*

# Our Final Chapter

*"I love you so much it hurts."*

—Mary

## A Difficult Decision

*"It's a good time to sell, and you will feel a huge weight lifted off your shoulders when you're out of debt," Robert said. "I'm not saying this because I'm your Realtor. I'm telling you because you're my friend."*

*Robert sold me the condo on Havenhurst Drive sixteen years ago. I asked him to stop by, and we discussed the housing market, my current expenses, and what price he thought my place would bring. Returning to full-time work provided a steady income, but I was struggling to keep my head above water. I had a mortgage, a second mortgage, and credit cards with high balances. I hated being in debt.*

*I knew selling my home was a good business decision, but how could I take Mac away from the only home he'd ever known? I loved our condo, our street, and our neighbors. Doing the right thing seemed so wrong.*

*To quote motivational speaker Tony Robbins, "Change happens when the pain of staying the same is greater than the pain of change." As much as I loved my home, the associated financial stress was overwhelming. Debt was making me ill, and I had access to a cure.*

*Once I made the decision to sell our house, I followed Robert's suggestions on how to make the place attractive to prospective buyers. Chairs went into storage, tchotchkes went in boxes, and even the piano was moved to a neighbor's house to make the condo look bigger. Painters covered scratches. Missing light bulbs were replaced. New plants took the place of dead ones.*

*Each change I made to prepare the house to sell seemed to suck the personality out of our home.*

🐾 🐾 🐾 🐾

I don't feel right. My tummy is nervous, and it hurts when I bark. It's dark when Mary picks me up at Nanny Nate's. I'm so tired when she comes to get me. I have to sit and rest a few times on the way home. I get to my house and there are boxes everywhere. My favorite chair is gone. Leashers come in and out to help Mary move things around. I wish I had the energy to let Mary know I don't like this.

*My first open house was a success. I got an offer on Saturday, accepted it on Sunday, and closed a week later. As apprehensive as I was to sell my house, things were falling into place. The new owners allowed Mac and me to stay in the condo for thirty days rent-free. My friend Artie offered me his guest house so I wouldn't have to rush to find a permanent home.*

*As soon as the money hit my account, I paid off every debt I had. Seeing "$0.00" on the credit cards and balances in the checking accounts was an amazing feeling. I was feeling lighter already. No more living paycheck to paycheck, and I had the savings that financial planners preach to have on hand in case of emergencies.*

*One came sooner than I expected, in the form of an $8,000 hospital bill.*

## Fashion Statement

*Mac is tough. He didn't let a broken leg deter him when he was eight months old, and he survived two mast cell tumors when he was seven. Last week's surgery was more serious. I almost lost him. But now he is home with me, where he is supposed to be. The large tumor on his heart is gone, and in true Celine Dion fashion, "His heart will go on."*

*I stare at Mac as he sleeps, gently stroking the thick fur on his back, and my heart is filled with gratitude. I think about that awful night when I visited him in the hospital after his surgery. IV tubes protruded from his shaved paws and the thick cords attached to his chest connected to beeping monitors. I called his name, and he slowly turned his head in my direction, staring past me through glazed eyes. He collapsed on the blankets and pillows that filled the heated kennel as if turning his head took all the energy he had. The nurses said I could stay if I wanted, but that Mac would be sleeping peacefully thanks to the lingering anesthetic and painkillers.*

*Although Mac was supposed to be in the hospital for three nights, he improved enough to be released after two. The doctor said he would need to be in a cone for several weeks, but Mac is a "no cone" kind of dog. Dr. Kim said a good option is T-shirts, so Mac became a post-surgical fashion statement on Havenhurst.*

*His favorite was a Golden State Warriors #30 Stephen Curry T-shirt, royal blue with gold lettering. If he was feeling tough, he wore his mixed martial arts T-shirt with local MMA champions Joban and Jackson emblazoned on the sleeves, black with yellow letters. Another favorite was the white America's Cup tee with a picture of a red and white sail boat when he was feeling particularly nautical.*

*Mac's wardrobe did more than take the place of an annoying cone. His apparel became a fun conversation piece for chats with neighbors.*

*The T-shirts elicited smiles and laughter in between the hugs and tears that invariably flowed when saying goodbye to our neighbors, our street family, our friends who would never go out of fashion.*

## Home in the Hills

Mary and I live in a house with no stairs. I get to go outside without Mary. I have a yard, and sometimes I get to stay outside all night long. I've found a corner where my adopted brothers Rocco and Tank can't find me. Their leasher Artie sees me but keeps it between us.

Rocco and Tank are Greater Swiss Mountain dogs. I don't know about the Swiss part, but they rise above me like great big mountains. The brothers fight to be close to me. Rocco gets on one side and Tank on the other, squeezing me in the middle. Mary calls us Oreo because their black fur presses against me, looking like the creamy white filling of those cookies she loves.

When Mary and Artie are at work, a leasher named Jesse takes Rocco and Tank on long walks. Since my heart surgery, I don't walk good, so Jesse leaves me in the yard while they're gone. Even when I'm inside, I feel like I'm outside because the front of our house is glass. I can sit on my sofa and see the city below like I used to see on our hikes in Runyon Canyon.

I miss my friends on my old street, but now Mary and I have a family. With Artie, Rocco, and Tank living next door and sharing my yard, Mary doesn't have to rely just on me for companionship.

When I was a puppy, I didn't like to share Mary. Now I think it's important that I do.

## Shutting Down

Mary doesn't understand. She thinks I'm strong, but I feel weak. Lying down is uncomfortable and standing up is tiring. My mouth feels like stuffed-animal stuffing is caught in my throat. Breathing is hard.

Mary brought a new leasher home with her today. His name is Kevin. He's nice and gentle and kind. He has a lot of stuff, so I hope he will stay for a while. Mary will need him.

She encourages me to get off the sofa. Getting down is not so bad. Gravity is on my side. I follow Mary and Kevin to the car. My body moves slowly, but my thoughts are jostling about in my head like a squirrel scurrying from tree to tree. She wants me to get in. I can't. Kevin is strong. He lifts me up into the back seat.

Rocco and Tank are in the SUV with Laura and Artie. There were too many of us to fit in one car. I'm glad about that. I love Rocco and Tank, but they don't understand that I don't feel like playing. We meet up on a tree-lined street in Beverly Hills. I can't tell what street it is because they are all tree-lined. Normally, I like coming here because the sidewalks are wide and the streets are flat. Rocco and Tank are excited for the walk, so they walk on. For Mary's sake, I try to follow. I'm at the end of the street. I know I'll never make it around the block so I stand at the corner. "What's wrong baby?" she says to me. "I don't know what's wrong with him," she says to Kevin. I can tell Mary is confused. I don't like disappointing her, but it's a long way around the block, and I'm too tired.

Kevin puts me back in the car and we go home. This will be my last car ride.

*I picked up my nephew Kevin at LAX and took him to Manhattan Beach for his first view of the Pacific Ocean. Kevin graduated from high school earlier this month, and his trip to California is my graduation present to him. I'm excited for Kevin to meet Mac. Most of my family lives in rural Virginia where dogs roam free on farms. After thirteen years of loving devotion to Mac, they've come to understand that he is more than a dog to me.*

*Mac greeted Kevin with a grin and a wagging tail but did not get off the sofa. Laura was visiting Artie and popped her head in the door to see if we wanted to join them for a walk in Beverly Hills. Rocco and Tank alone fill up Artie's SUV, so I said we'd meet them there. Mac seemed content to stay on the sofa and had to be coaxed out the door. When we met up with Artie and Laura, the dogs were already leashed and ready to walk. Mac was moving slowly, so I told them to go on. Kevin and I walked in place to mimic Mac's pace. I bent down to hug Mac and buried my face in the thick fur of his neck. "What's wrong baby?" I told Kevin, "I don't know what's wrong with him." We called it a night as Kevin lifted Mac into the back seat.*

*I took the week off and had lots of activities planned—Universal Studios, The Late Late Show with James Corden, Jimmy Kimmel Live, and Disneyland.*

*My phone was on airplane mode while we were at The Late Late Show, which is taped not-so-late at 4:00 p.m. As we walked to the car that Tuesday night, I turned the phone back on to multiple texts and voicemails from Artie asking me to call him. My chest tightened as shaking fingers dialed Artie's number. A panicked voice answered.*

*"Mac has shit himself on the sofa. He can't walk. His gagging has gotten worse." We rushed home to see Mac lying in his feces. He couldn't stand up. He lifted his head and tried to clear his throat, sounding like an old man just before he spits.*

*I kissed the bridge of his nose and stroked his back. He lay still as I lifted each leg to clean him while Kevin and Artie slid out the soiled sheet from under his body and replaced it with a clean one. No one said a word. I looked into Mac's eyes and he seemed resigned. Once he was clean, Mac closed his eyes to rest.*

*I walked outside to the fence where Artie was staring at the lighted skyline of downtown Los Angeles. He turned around and I collapsed into his tight hug. My body was shaking, and I was crying uncontrollably. "I know baby. This is so hard. You love him so much, but this is not quality of life." He continued saying what I'm sure were kind words, but I heard nothing, only the voice inside me saying I had to let Mac go.*

*I left a message for Mac's vet, Peter, who I knew was in Hawaii. Peter called as soon as he got my message. "The gagging could mean his larynx is paralyzed. The next step would be to put a scope down his throat, but we'd have to put him under." I knew Peter was giving me options, but we both knew what needed to happen. I was not going to put Mac through another surgery. Once I vocalized this to Peter, he said, "Mary, Paul and I will be back in town Thursday for twenty-two hours, and then we leave for the East Coast for two weeks. I could come to the house Thursday morning."*

## Saying Goodbye

The pain in my body is stronger than my ability to hide it from Mary. She knows. That's why she's been sleeping on the hard floor beside my bed for the last two nights. She's tired. I am, too. So many leashers have come to say goodbye. I hope they hear my silent pleas to take care of Mary when I'm gone. The only part of my body that feels normal is my eyes. I try to comfort Mary with my stare.

*Peter explained beforehand how the process works. He will give Mac a sedative, and then when he feels Mac's body relax, he'll inject the euthanasia drug that shuts down his heart and brain functions within one or two minutes. We can be with him for as long as we want. There will be a man in a truck backed up at the gate who will carry Mac away in a sled-like carrier with three sides.*

*I don't remember any of this. I was in a fog from grief and lack of sleep. I can't believe that less than a week ago, Mac was healthy and active. As I look back to Saturday night, I realize that he was shutting down. I didn't know it then. I knew that it was odd for him not to want to walk around the block with Rocco and Tank. I'm grateful that he didn't suffer long and that I didn't have to wonder if I was doing the right thing. Mac made it easy on me. He even managed to leave this earth in the twenty-two hours that his beloved vet Peter was in town.*

*What I do remember is that his passing was peaceful. He was surrounded by friends and family, lying on the flowered Laura Ashley comforter that we shared many naps on. He was in the yard that he so enjoyed the last ten months of his life, looking down over a city of parks where he had played, restaurants where he'd eaten, and Starbucks where he licked dry cups of whipped cream.*

*I remember thinking it was a wonderful way to die and how I wished it could be that way for leashers, too.*

## The Perfect Dog

*Two days ago, you went to be with Jesus. I didn't want to let you go, but I had to. I couldn't let you suffer anymore. I knew the day was fast approaching. Before you left, I wanted to have that perfect day you read about.*

*I wanted to take you to the park on the street where you grew up so all your friends could say goodbye. I wanted to take you to the beach to smell the waves you craved as a puppy. I wanted to take you for steak and ice cream. I wanted the perfect day.*

*But you were too weak. Only your eyes were alert. They told me, "Mary, I don't need the perfect day. I've had the perfect life. I'm ready to go. Tell me you'll be okay. I love you."*

*Rest in peace, my dear sweet Mac.*

# Thank You for Being My Friend

*"I think people who don't believe in soulmates just haven't met the right animal yet."*

—Quote from an Emily McDowell Studio greeting card

## Thank You Mac

*Thank you for being the reason I walk two miles every morning.*

*Thank you for being why I don't stay out until two in the morning and have that extra cocktail or two.*

*Thank you for introducing me to beautiful people and dogs everywhere we go.*

*Thank you for being the warm body in my bed that I can put my arm around when no one else is there.*

*Thank you for being my greeting committee each time I walk in the door and for making me feel like a queen in a world that's not always so regal.*

*Thank you for protecting me from the statue at the park or the garbage truck that barrels down the street on Tuesday.*

*Thank you for growling at the man who doesn't seem like he'd be good for me.*

*Thank you for not covering your ears in disgust when I sing or at least try to.*

*Thank you for your big brown eyes that look at me with the understanding of a sage and for your sloppy wet tongue that kisses me when I cry and sometimes when I don't.*

*Thank you for making me laugh when you do things you're not supposed to, like jumping on me each time I lie on the floor to do sit-ups or trying to get under me when I do push-ups.*

*Thank you for eating the skin off the chicken so I don't.*

*Thank you for the joy you bring me when I see how much fun you have running into the ocean after a ball. It is truly one of my favorite things in life.*

*Thank you for introducing me to a life that is different than the one I had before you came along.*

*Thank you for being the inspiration for this book.*

## I Love You

Mary, I love you. You say it so many times to me. I say it to you many times, too. But my voice is different than yours.

When I hear the turn of your tires in the garage, my body says I love you when I sit at the top of the stairs waiting for you to open the door.

When you come into the house, my feet say I love you when I bring you my favorite toy because seeing you is my joy.

When we wake up, my morning stretch says I love you because I know you like to rub my tummy.

When we watch television on the sofa, cuddling says I love you and don't want you to get up, unless you're getting me something to eat.

When we go on walks, my insistence to stay outside says I love you because you need to interact with other leashers.

When you look sad, my tongue says I love you by licking your face until you laugh and you're not sad anymore.

When I hear someone on the sidewalk, my bark says I love you and I'm here to protect you because...

I am the Man of the House, and always will be.

# Afterword

It will soon be two years since I said good-bye to Mac. It doesn't seem that long. I talk to him every day and think of him constantly. When I leave the house, I say goodbye to the symbolic him, a heavy bronze heart holding his ashes. Some days I place my hand in his paw imprinted on a five-inch round white plaster of Paris disc. At night I hug a pillow with his name on it. I'm not as sad as I used to be. I've learned to live with the hole in my heart.

The first month was hell, and I cried relentlessly. I had no purpose. The first "everything" triggered a torrent of tears. The first time I ate an individual container of Greek yogurt and Mac wasn't there to lick it clean. The first time I went to Trader Joe's and saw a pack of "Just Chicken." Seeing someone I hadn't seen since he died was especially difficult.

A raw and unexpected moment occurred when I stopped to get a tuna sandwich at Ice Cream and More, a small unassuming shop in a dated strip center at the top of the street where we used to live. Mr. Kim, a polite and reserved Korean man, is the owner. As soon as I opened the door, tears welled up in my eyes. I didn't say a word. Pain is a language of its own. Mr. Kim came out from behind the freezer that contained colorful homemade ice creams, sorbets, and yogurts. He hugged me tight and with tears in his eyes said, "Mac was such a good dog."

I found solace spreading Mac's ashes in the places he loved most—the top of Runyon Canyon, the jagged rocks in the ocean at

Malibu where we rested before walking back to our car, and along the sidewalk at our condo where he chased tennis balls for hours. I still have some of his ashes in a small Ziploc bag. He was a big boy, so there were a lot of ashes.

The 1955 convertible Thunderbird sat idle for months. I rarely drove it without him as co-pilot. He got so much attention sitting in the passenger side of the teal-and-white bench seat with his head sticking over the side of the car door, feeling the wind in his face. I have great pictures of him in that car, and so do many others. Strangers would ask if they could take a photo of Mac in the T-bird. We once were videotaped for over a mile driving down Sunset Boulevard.

Going places without Mac was and still is hard. It's no fun eating alone at restaurants. I usually defer to takeout. Recently several of our favorite restaurants have gone out of business. It's harder to hold on to the memories when the physical places where we made them are gone.

I'm frequently asked whether I will get another dog. My go-to answer is, "I have Arturo's dogs next door. If it wasn't for them, I would probably have one already." I'm not sure that's true, but it's what I tell people, and myself.

When I was younger, I dreamed of marriage and children. Mac taught me that family doesn't mean you have to get married and motherhood doesn't require having children. Chinese philosopher Lao Tzu is quoted, "When the student is ready, the teacher appears." Mac was my teacher. He taught me how to be a Mom. He taught me to love and care for a dog. He introduced me to the dog community where I will always be welcome. Lao Tzu goes on to say, "When the student is truly ready, the teacher disappears." It will soon be time to show another dog what my teacher, Mac Headley Kiser, taught me.

# Acknowledgments

I want to first acknowledge The Learning Annex that advertised its courses in newspaper format available in stands throughout Los Angeles. Though no longer in business, The Learning Annex offered classes in everything from acting to horseback riding to belly dancing and, thankfully, writing. It was through The Learning Annex that I took a writing class taught by Jim Martyka.

Without Jim, this book would not have been finished, much less published. Jim kept in touch with me for years to see how *Man of the House* was coming along. He believed in my voice (and Mac's) even when I didn't. Thank you Jim for your patience, edits, advice, and persistence. You are a talented professional and a genuinely great guy.

I want to thank Marilyn Friedman and Jeff Bernstein and their brainchild Writing Pad for giving me the writing bug. I'm so glad that I answered the *Daily Candy* ad and showed up at your lovely Silverlake home for a five-week tasting menu with courses in poetry, prose, fiction, nonfiction, and memoir. Telling me what you liked and what you remembered about my stories gave me the courage to continue writing.

I want to thank Joey Scott for reading what I thought was my final draft and making me realize I was strong enough to write "Our Final Chapter."

If Mac were here, he would thank Lisa Headley who was a second mom to him and taught him how to speak. He'd thank Blake Seaton for puppy sitting when he was too young for daycare and not minding when he shed on the purple sofa. He would thank Arturo Barquet for giving him a yard and a view of the city for the last ten months of his life.

Thank you to all the doctors who cared for Mac: Drs. Hiebert, Turner, Carey, and the wonderful staff at Access Specialty Animal Hospital in Culver City, but most of all, Dr. Patrick Mahaney, a friend and neighbor, who cared for Mac and treated him as his own.

Heartfelt thanks to my amazing neighbors on Havenhurst Drive in West Hollywood. You are all that is good about community. Our walks and talks were the inspiration for this book.

I want to thank my family—my Mom for being the least materialistic person on Earth, always reminding me that "pretty is as pretty does," and teaching me to live courageously and independently by her example; my sister Lucy for rejoicing in my successes and still believing in me when I failed; and my brother Dean for teaching me to play poker when I was 10 years old, and for being there for family when I'm so far away. Thank you to my many nieces and nephews for being such diverse but amazing human beings and for taking care of me when I'm old. Thank you to my sister Linda whose name I cannot type without tears flowing down my cheeks. You were an angel on earth who was taken from us way too soon. No one would have loved this book more or been prouder of me. You were a great writer. The hand-written notes and letters you sent me throughout my life is such a lost art. I miss them and I miss you.

Last, but certainly not least, thank you to my chosen family. You know who you are. My life did not take the traditional turn that I thought it would, but if it had, I would not have met you.

# About the Author

Mary Kiser grew up in the Shenandoah Valley of Virginia but now calls Los Angeles home, where she is a Senior Vice President at Bank of America. During a hiatus from banking, she began writing a journal from her dog Mac's point of view. The book lay unfinished until she was compelled to keep a deathbed promise to her 13-year-old yellow lab to complete their story.

When not working or writing, Mary loves hiking and spending time with friends in the southern California sunshine.

Made in the USA
Las Vegas, NV
18 December 2020

13729092R00146